ESCAPE UNDER SAIL

PURSUE YOUR LIVEABOARD DREAM

ESCAPE UNDER SAIL

PURSUE YOUR LIVEABOARD DREAM

Leonard Skinner
and Mary Cooney

ADLARD
COLES

LONDON · OXFORD · NEW YORK · NEW DELHI · SYDNEY

Dedicated to Bill and Laurel Cooper, whose generosity of time and knowledge has ignited the dreams of a thousand liveaboards.

'We were dreamers once. Dreams can become a reality. It is hard work, rather than magic, that gets it done.'
Bill and Laurel Cooper, authors of Sell Up and Sail

ADLARD COLES
Bloomsbury Publishing Plc
50 Bedford Square, London, WC1B 3DP, UK

BLOOMSBURY, ADLARD COLES and the Adlard Coles logo are trademarks of Bloomsbury Publishing Plc

First published in Great Britain 2019

A catalogue record for this book is available from the British Library

Library of Congress Cataloguing-in-Publication data has been applied for.

ISBN: 978-1-4729-5926-3; ePDF: 978-1-4729-5924-9; ePub: 978-1-4729-5925-6
2 4 6 8 10 9 7 5 3 1

Typeset by Deanta Global Publishing Services, Chennai, India
Printed and bound in India by Replika Press Pvt. Ltd.

To find out more about our authors and books visit
www.bloomsbury.com and sign up for our newsletters

Contents

Contents

Foreword

Thirty years on (and more) from writing *Sell Up and Sail,* I am still contacted by people happily cruising long or short distances, saying, 'You and Bill were our inspiration', or 'It's all your fault!'

One such couple was Leonard and Mary, who several years ago, while over for the Boat Show from Ireland, asked to come and see us. They were at the beginning of their escape under sail, and had some questions to ask. When I learned recently that they had written a book that might answer those and many more questions and would like me to look at it with a view to writing a foreword, I was seized with panic. Was this going to be a *Sell Up and Sail* lookalike, desperately needed as it was?

I need not have worried. Leonard and Mary are their own people, and both strong characters. The framework of the book has to be similar because of the ground to be covered, but while many seagoing issues are still the same after centuries, much has changed in the last 30 years.

When we wrote our book there was no internet, GPS, social media or smartphones. Communication was by letter or frustrating sessions in hot phone boxes with a weighty pile of coins. Navigation was by eyeball, sextant, paper charts and the seat of our pants. In mid-ocean, weather reports were hard to come by except from passing ships.

Leonard and Mary provide up-to-date chapters on navigation by electronic chart, using GPS and AIS, useful apps for your smartphone (what a blessing that is for today's sailors), and whether a TV is a useful addition, as well as traditional skills that don't change, such as knots, rigging, first aid for long-distance cruisers, weather forecasting, anchoring, storing ship, cooking and catering. They are home schooling their two teenage children as they sail, and their words of wisdom on that topic are an invaluable addition to the book.

They also have a great deal of advice on what it will cost. In today's climate it is harder to budget than it was in our day (we had a big house to sell and Bill's naval pension as a back-up), so these chapters will be of great help to today's escapees, always remembering that what it will cost depends on what you want for your money, and that is as long as a piece of string.

Also covered is the inevitable occasional clash between two (or more) opinionated and intelligent people trying to get along in a smaller space than they have been used to. Finding out how much you enjoy the cruising life — the discoveries, the excitement, the healthy environment, the instant companionship with the boat next door, and, yes, the occasional moments of danger successfully overcome — all help to get past the hurdles and pitfalls. I look back on the many years and many miles of cruising with Bill with immense happiness, and memories both wonderful and heart-stopping.

Here it is, thanks to Leonard and Mary of *Faoin Spéir,* long awaited and much needed, a worthy successor to *Sell Up and Sail.*

Laurel Cooper, 2019

Introduction

 So, is this another book about how someone bought an old boat and sailed off into the sunset? That's certainly how it started out but it grew into a catalogue of all that we've learned along the way. The easy lessons and, more importantly, the hard ones. It started with a simple conversation around the kitchen table one evening, and continues with us living and cruising on a sailboat, without it costing the world. Before we get started (and I'd like to think that this is part of the draw of this adventure), we should point out that when we began, we were not experts in anything to do with sailing or boats. What we write on this topic has been learned from books, from other sailors who were generous with their time, or good old-fashioned trial and error. What we are pretty good at, perhaps, is seeing ways through difficulties and executing plans that others might deem impossible.

It will be useful to note that Mary and I (Leonard) write with independence throughout the book. That is to say, we don't always agree on how things should be done. And you'll know who's writing at any one time because you'll see an  for Leonard and an  for Mary.

In all seriousness though, one of the most wonderful things about escaping under sail and sustaining a life on a sailboat is that no two people do it in exactly the same way. So even on the same boat, people have different (sometimes wildly different) ideas about the same experience, and it's important to recognise that each idea is as valid as the other, for wouldn't life be rather boring if we all found the same meaning in every experience?

To the superhumans, the racers and the endurance athletes, you have my utmost admiration – just don't expect us to keep up. We have found that, for us, 'sailing around the world' actually translates to 'sailing *about* the world'. Moving from port to port as and when the mood takes us, sometimes we stop for a day, sometimes for six months. Liveaboard cruising is as varied a lifestyle as the personalities who engage in it. If you do everything that we do, one of us is doing it wrong. Once you've read this book and the many other excellent publications available, remember the lessons but do your own thing regardless.

Ⓜ When Leonard and I set out to become liveaboards we had no idea what it would really entail. We read other cruisers' books on how they managed to achieve a similar goal. We didn't follow any one of these exactly; instead we read and distilled from each what might suit us or be relevant to our path to the liveaboard lifestyle. I know that these days everybody searches the internet for the solution to everything, but I have more faith in the written word. What I hope you find in these pages is our unique perspective in terms of our particular experience. We have achieved a cruising lifestyle on a budget, and although we are very explicit in sharing figures with you, they are *our* figures and no two boats are the same. We do believe, however, that the cruising lifestyle can be achieved on any budget. It is also our belief that it is possible for anybody to develop the skill set required for cruising, but allowing yourself the time to practise is necessary. We started, genuinely, with nothing – no experience, no money and no sailing skills – and we want to encourage people who are in the same position as us to achieve their goals.

There are two noteworthy points about starting from scratch: first, you do find your own way, and second, when you find your own way into sailing you have to trust your own instincts, too. There is a significant amount of horse manure that abounds in the yachting world; it would be a great pity to let that put you off when you encounter it, but encounter it you will. Contrary to popular belief you do not need a certain type of product on your boat to make it safe; you do not need a certain type of jacket or pair of shoes to sail and feel the wind in your hair and the freedom of the high seas. All you need is a seaworthy boat, a sound understanding of tides, currents and winds, an awareness of health and safety, and a level of competence for manoeuvring the boat safely. All of this is achievable with time, patience and practice, and to anybody who wants it and is willing to work hard and learn. The yachting world is also filled with kind, supportive and generous people who are eager to share their experience and skill, and it is useful to take every opportunity to learn from them. However, one of the main reasons we wrote this book is to encourage those who are just starting out to learn what they can from as many sources as possible and to value their own judgement, too.

We initially wrote this book to catalogue our journey into the cruising lifestyle. It explores the avenues we took to finding information and how we made sense of that information for ourselves. It is not intended to be a guidebook. Rather, it offers possibilities and you must make the choices that suit you and your family to achieve your own goals, which you must set. I firmly believe this to be a crucial piece of the puzzle: finding your own path and following it. The key to doing this is figuring out what it is you want by asking the right questions. That may seem pretty obvious, and it is not my wish to insult anybody, but it is worth taking the time to clarify what you want to achieve and how you imagine you will get there in concrete steps.

A note for couples

It is important to note that as a couple, if you are a couple, you may not be in the same place at the outset, that you may in fact want totally different things. It is worth considering how you both feel about that revelation.

What matters, though, is that you talk, talk, talk, openly and honestly. If there are things that cause you to fight or disagree, or perhaps one of you to zone out, those are exactly the things you need to be discussing. Have those conversations! The process of coming to a joint decision need not be harmonious but it does need to happen.

As Leonard mentioned, we are writing with independent voices. We want to do this for a variety of reasons but primarily because we think it might empower couples who read our book to realise that sometimes we agree wholeheartedly with each other, sometimes we disagree profoundly, but that we can still follow our dream and build a life together and be deeply in love. In addition, we do this on a 39-foot sailboat, which we share with my teenaged twins, and we make it work.

1

In the beginning

What kind of family ends up living on a boat, sailing about the world? You may be pleasantly surprised to find that we are actually quite average people who come from non-sailing kin. We are proof that you don't have to have spent your preschool days sailing an optimist dinghy to follow the dream of liveaboard cruising. In truth, very few liveaboards that we meet have such backgrounds.

Meet the crew

As a small child, I lived in the army barracks in Cobh on the south coast of Ireland, and we had the most amazing view out over Cork harbour. Cobh, or 'Queenstown' as it was known historically, was the last port of call for the ill-fated *Titanic* and it has a long seafaring tradition – a tradition in which I had no part. My father was an army man from Tralee and my mother a homemaker from Cork city. Neither had any inclination towards the sea. In fact, my father had quite an aversion to it, and I don't know of a single relative who had ever gone to sea or even messed around on small boats until my brother joined the Irish navy.

From the kitchen window in our army house, the entire harbour and all that went on there was visible. It was 1970s Ireland, and although the town of Crosshaven, at the mouth of the harbour, was host to the Royal Cork Yacht Club, I don't remember seeing a single yacht. What I loved to watch from my windowsill perch were the big ships coming in. The harbour control building and pilot boats were just below our house and I could see the pilot race out to the ships and make the precarious transfer before guiding them into port. Then the tugs would go about their business, pulling and pushing, nudging and prodding the behemoths into position. Perhaps it was this early reality TV show that played out before me that led to a lifelong niggling in the back of my mind that I'd like to be out on the water.

When I was six, we moved from Cobh to Tralee, and all I could see from any of the windows in the house were more houses. I spent the first chapter of my adult working life in the electronics industry. Throughout this time, I never lost my love of the sea, and at age 34 I decided it was time to learn to sail. In my usual style, instead of spending a thousand pounds on a sailing course, I felt it prudent to spend £1,200 on a boat and figure it out as I went.

Now, I was not a fool. I had taken a lesson. Well, sort of. The University of Limerick, where I had been teaching, had a staff sailing club and had offered a free taster evening. I jumped at the chance and went out with five others in a Wayfarer dinghy for two hours on a windless evening. We drifted along finding the occasional puff of wind while I made a mental note of everything that was going on. I remembered the ropes and how they ran. I listened to every word and at the end of our two-hour drift in a sailing dinghy, we paddled back to shore and I was ready to buy and sail a yacht of my own across the vast expanse that is Lough Derg, a beautiful lake on Ireland's well-served inland waterways.

As unusual as it may sound, the first 'yacht' I had ever set foot on was my own, and what a boat she was, all 17 foot of her. A bilge-keel 'Pirate Express' from the early 1980s and a trailer that had seen better days. Essentially, learning to sail meant going out on the lake and hoisting the jib, tracking over and back, taking in the jib, hoisting the main and tracking over and back some more. 'Easy-peasy', or so I thought, until I put up both sails together and felt like the whole boat was going to capsize any second! I opted for a more gradual learning curve after that, and even today my preference is to cruise along at a sedate 5 knots rather than risk spilling my tea.

M I grew up inland but, like Leonard, I loved the sea, or maybe I loved to walk on the beach close to the sea! As a child, I enjoyed school and learning. I always knew I would leave my hometown as soon as I could. Don't get me wrong, I liked where I grew up but I knew there was lots more to see, much more to visit and heaps more to learn.

17

As an 18-year-old I couldn't wait to spread my wings and fly. And so I did.

I entered a convent and became a nun for 10 years. Not exactly adventure, I hear you say, but it did provide me with a chance to live with some very well-educated and wise women who taught me the merits of tolerance, patience, valuing experience and reflecting on it, and, most importantly, the values of simplicity and living in the present moment.

I left the convent in my mid-20s and for the next 12 years or so I lived the single life. I had a good job, holidayed abroad a lot and bought a house. I trained as a therapist and improved my professional life by developing skill sets that made me a valuable member of the workforce.

Luke and Ella, my children, now serve as competent crew, mast climbers and general hi-jinksers on board. Born together in 2003, they've probably had the steepest learning curve of the four of us. Although we decided to take on this project in late 2011, it was almost two years before we mentioned anything to them (or anyone else for that matter). Now 14 years old, it's as though living on a boat is the most normal thing in the world to Luke and Ella.

When I met Leonard he was living on a lake on his own boat, a tiny sailboat that he had taught himself to sail. I remember the first time I sailed in that boat; it was truly terrifying! But we will return to my being scared of sailing later in the book. Leonard and I became friends, dated and finally we moved in together. Leonard is a great one for ideas and plans and going for it. One night towards the end of 2011, we were sitting at the kitchen table drinking tea and he said to me, 'Mary, do you fancy sailing around the world?' and I said 'Yes'. And thus began the *Faoin Spéir* project, which has since become our family living aboard an old sailboat, sailing about the world. I hope I am not making it sound like it happened magically because believe me when I say that it's been hard work to get to this place – but more on that later.

Faoin Spéir

Enough about the crew. For us, the star of the show is *Faoin Spéir* (pronounced 'Fween Spare'). The final protagonist in our story is also middle-aged, having come to life in 1976 at Hank McCune's boatyard in California, USA. Hank, curiously, was the host of a popular TV show from the 1950s that bore his name. *Faoin Spéir* was one of the centre cockpit Yorktown 39s his boatyard produced. According to our reading, the yard sold the boats as bare-hull kits and supplied workspace and advice for customer completion. Of course, this means that the layout and standard of work varied greatly. Not that it made any difference to us, as we found our boat completely stripped out. Before reaching us, she had sailed the length of the Pacific coast of North and Central America, from Alaska to Panama. From there, she went all the way up to Boston, where she crossed the North Atlantic to Ireland for a few years of cruising about Northern Europe.

Faoin Spéir looking dapper in Newlyn, Cornwall, England.

This heritage is so very reassuring when out at sea and the chop becomes uncomfortable. To know that the boat has seen and done it all before, and has many years sailing left in her is a comfort. After all, wouldn't it be a shame for her to travel all this way and not complete the circle!

Faoin Spéir: the specs

For the 'boat nerds' out there (of which I am one), here are *Faoin Spéir*'s specs:

Hull type: Encapsulated long-fin keel

LOA: 39ft (11.88m)

LWL: 33ft (10m)

Beam: 11ft 8in (3.6m)

Displacement: 15,000lb

Ballast: 7,000lb

Dry weight (unloaded): 9,000kg

Rig type: Masthead sloop

Engine: 35 HP Chrysler Nissan four-cylinder diesel

Transmission: 1:1 Borg Warner into a two-blade prop

Mast height: 42ft (12.8m)

Layout

Because of the bare nature of the hull, we had a blank canvas on which to work. The layout suits us well as a liveaboard family of four with regular visitors.

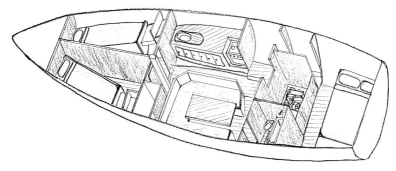

Faoin Spéir: the layout

Our starting point

At the beginning of our quest to become liveaboard cruisers, we really did start from zero. Not just financially; our collective experience, knowledge and understanding of exactly what 'liveaboard cruiser' entails amounted to nothing. I had read some articles and had occasionally heard reports about people who had 'given it all up' to 'sail off into the sunset'. But our reality was that we had nothing more than a fleeting, romanticised view of what that meant. With this in mind, we will assume that at least some of you are coming from the same place, so forgive us if some of what we cover appears simplistic.

The truth is that the entire venture is simplistic. That is to say that it is a venture where the end goal is one of simplicity. Throughout the journey, when faced with a choice, we invariably went for the simpler option. The benefits are many, but primarily it is usually the cheaper solution and the easier one to learn, and so I went straight to the books and magazines. I read prolifically from those who had gone before. Over time I built up an idea in my head of what it meant to be a liveaboard cruising sailor. Of course, now that we are on the other side of the project and are actually living the life, I realise that if I really knew nothing starting out, it was just a little more than nothing by the time we had permanently slipped the lines.

The big question that most people have from day one – as in the very moment they seriously consider following that dream – is 'how much does it cost?' Perhaps the reason why this question is so common is that nobody can answer it. Everyone has a different answer, and in all the books I've read, large sums of money do appear to be needed. Whether it's a case of selling your house to set sail, or cashing in your pension, or, as mentioned in several other books, tending to your stock market investments. I recall one 'budget' book (to be fair, it is an excellent one) talking about a 'tiny budget' of £40,000! I can tell you now that you do not need such large sums to follow this path. Obviously some money is needed but not as much as you think if you are prepared to put in the time and effort. Essentially, I believe that this lifestyle can be achieved on any budget – we did it for about the price of a second-hand car. We didn't have a lump sum, so the costs were broken down over the four years we worked on the project. If you can, imagine getting a car loan (an activity best kept in the realm of fantasy) for £10,000, not an unreasonable size of loan for a car in this modern world of buy, buy, buy, latest, new, flashy. Let's skip the interest to keep things simple, so that over four years the cost is £2,500 per year, or about £50 per week. This is a manageable figure for pretty much anyone living in a modern Western society. For those who are crying out, '£50 a week! Easy for you to say!', believe me when I say that these cries are loudest in my own head. The question is, what are you willing to give up in order to achieve your goal? Do you take a holiday each year? Do you enjoy a drink on a Friday night? What about that takeaway pizza? Or let's get really gritty – do you have a car and how badly do you really need it?

The key is really the first £500, for with a sum as small as this you can buy a 20-foot sailboat that needs a good scrub and a little (or sometimes a lot) of sealant. This will get you sailing and help you to understand the bits that you like or dislike about your boat and spending time on the water.

But, I fear we're getting ahead of ourselves. If, like us, you are beginning from zero, start reading. Find out as much as you can. Get to the library or get online. Start with the classics – Joshua Slocum, Bernard Moitessier, Robin Knox-Johnston. All of these authors write from a time before GPS, wind instruments and onboard microwave ovens. Simple, reliable craft and simple, reliable techniques. There are also many things to be learned from magazine articles, but quite often they are filled with suggestions for modern equipment, which may serve only to fill your boat and deplete your budget. Become informed, read, ask questions, visit boats. Do something every day that takes you a little bit closer to achieving your goal. I know that sounds like a cliché but it worked for us. For example, keep a couple of metre-long lengths of rope around the house. When you're sitting on the sofa watching TV, pick up a rope and tie a couple of bowlines while the ads are on. Or while you're sitting in the bathtub, tie a rolling hitch on to the tap. This not only improves your rope skills, which are vital to life on a sailboat, but it also focuses your mind a little more each day. It reminds you of your goal. You might even start to see yourself as a liveaboard cruising sailor long before you actually move on to a boat.

This is fundamental to succeeding. You have to transition from the life that you have grown up with (the life that most people see as normal and usual) into your new liveaboard cruising self. Having a boat is merely part of the endgame, but becoming the sort of person who moves on to a boat and spends their life sailing around the world requires no boat or budget at all. It only requires the will to challenge what you are used to, and to become the person you want to be. I recall a wonderful quote – I wish I knew who first wrote it: 'Don't try to find yourself, create yourself.'

M We made our plan and broke it down into very practical steps. We planned for everything. In truth, what we wanted at the beginning was to escape to a life less usual, and I am not entirely sure we even knew what that meant. I saw it as hanging out in hot places with white sandy beaches and clear blue water, but inevitably, the goals became more refined as our plan progressed.

We told no one at first because we wanted to get used to the idea ourselves. Based on the response we got when we did share our news, I would advise prospective liveaboards to be as solid as they can be about their intentions before they do so. Very few in our circle of friends and relatives embraced the idea without reservation or supported us wholeheartedly. Be prepared to defend your position and explain it over and over again. From a psychological point of view, I get it – our choice was outside the norm. It was scary for our friends and family because they feared for our lives. They recognised that we had limited sailing experience and they were right. They believed that we were taking unnecessary risks – not only with our own lives, but also Luke and Ella's. Another belief was that we were taking foolish risks with the children's educational futures and cutting them off from their friends and support networks. All of the above are reasonable points and they certainly demand due consideration. It is therefore advisable to anybody considering a cruising lifestyle to leave enough time between announcing your plan and your departure date to allow for these important conversations with loved ones; it's essential for everyone's mental health and peace of mind. I would say, though, that the point is not to assuage or placate people or make everything all right. You are entitled to make a choice that is out of the ordinary and your family and friends will accept it eventually.

There are uncomfortable realities about choosing an alternative lifestyle. It challenges many people's thinking about how they live their lives and that can make for uneasy relationships. I have met numerous people who have taken time out of their lives to travel and they have reaped enormous benefits from it. In fact, I don't know a single person who has regretted it.

I struggled with the reactions of others, but in hindsight I was probably naive. The reactions were at worst negative and at best sceptical. The thing that threw me the most though was the belief – held by many – that we were 'mad' or 'daft'. It felt like everybody else was doing the right thing by their children and I was making choices that would leave them scarred for life, and socially or educationally disadvantaged. The truth is that I don't know what is right or wrong. I do not even believe there is a right or wrong. I believe all parents make the best decisions and choices for their children and hope for the best outcome. Generally, parents have the same struggles whatever the circumstances of their lives. The important thing is to consider what you value for your children, what kind of people you want them to be and then set goals that will help them to achieve this. I believe it is critical to challenge yourself as a parent and to rethink your decisions and choices over and over as your children develop. I am pretty sure that process can happen wherever, or however, you live.

I should say that at this point we did not include Ella and Luke in the initial stages of planning. I felt they were too young and we first needed to get our own heads around the processes of moving from land to sea. Placing them in a morass of unknown variables would put them in a position of few certainties and raise unnecessary anxieties. Our plan at the beginning was to move on board the summer they finished primary school, which would allow for them to complete their primary education and facilitate an easier transition with less emotional trauma. That was the hope, anyway. However, we did include them before we told anybody else. We also told Leonard's son, David, at the same time and made it clear that he was free to join us if he wished to do so. David was 20 and a career musician. He opted not to take us up on our offer but does regularly join us on board for some downtime.

Through my research, I moved from a situation in which I knew nothing about sailing and sailboats to a place where I had a fairly decent working understanding. I tried to find people who I could relate to, who understood even partially what I was experiencing. My overwhelming emotional state was anxiety in the beginning – feeling out of control and scared. But my life philosophy is to feel something, then make sense of it and understand it, and in that awareness to try to do something about it. I did do something: I wrote in my journal. I asked questions. I looked for answers. After we bought the boat, I moaned about how uncomfortable it was and how uncomfortable I felt in it, but I continued to return to it most weekends. As I spent time there and slowly adapted to this discomfort, I challenged myself to explore how it could become a home. Why did I put myself through all this? Looking back now, it does seem like a bit of a nightmare. I did it because I really wanted this life and I had to face up to the reality of what I felt if I wanted it to work. In addition, I could not support my children to make the transition unless I was prepared to make it myself.

I want to be very clear that I did none of this by myself. I wrecked poor Leonard's head with my whining and moaning. I had sessions with my therapist of many years and I talked the ears off my sisters and countless friends. In my humble opinion, it is essential to talk through what's going on for you – the good, the bad and the ugly. Pretending you are fine when you are a mess just makes things so much worse, so try to be honest with yourself and share your feelings as kindly as you can with your partner so they are fully aware of what it is you're going through. In my experience, there is a way to manage anything together but I have not yet met somebody who can read minds. Talking and sharing is the key.

2
Why do we do it?

L If humankind had not evolved the desire to roam the world, the chances are I would not be here writing this. We would never have moved beyond the horizon and would have died off after exhausting the resources in the area of our birth. Explaining 'why' we feel this need can make for interesting discussion, and it is often brought up by those trying to 'cure' themselves – or indeed others – of their wanderlust.

Charles Darwin told us the characteristics that lead to procreation are those most likely to lead to surviving to adulthood. Put simply, if a person has a trait that makes them a better survivor, they are likely to have offspring who are more likely to survive. The desire to move beyond our immediate locality is one such trait, a trait that has led humankind to cover the globe. As a species, we could not support a population of 7 billion in some valley in Ethiopia, and so survival was dependent on our distant ancestors setting out beyond the horizon. If our natural inclination is to move on and live a nomadic lifestyle, then the real question is not 'Why do we go?', but rather 'Why *don't* we go?'

The obvious answer is that modern life is such that all our needs can be satisfied locally. Secure housing, education and employment are within easy reach for most of us. Within a few clicks of a mouse, someone in the local supermarket is filling a trolley with my shopping, which will soon arrive at my door. I'm left with the question, 'Why is this better than walking to the shop myself?' Our brains have a tendency to try to keep us safe in order to help us survive. If I stay close to home and go to work each morning and do my shopping in the same familiar store, no harm will come of me. Who knows what ills may befall me if I holiday in a new country, much less set off to sea in a small boat. And so our brains tell us to stay put. The ultimate version of this quest for safety might be to move as little as possible from your bedroom, work from home and order everything that you need online to be delivered to your door. You could walk 5 miles a day on a treadmill in your room and eat a healthy balanced diet. This is, of course, fine for many but, for me, the reality of this would be a life not worth living. As morbid as it may sound, death comes to us all eventually and I'm fine with trading a few years of old age for a more fulfilling middle bit.

Life on a cruising sailboat is a way of regaining a little independence. It's an exercise in rediscovering the multi-skilled lifestyle for which we have evolved. I choose to live in a way that taxes all the attributes my ancestors developed. I love nothing more than the smell of fresh seafood cooking on the boat while I dry myself off after having caught it. I simply do not feel the same satisfaction popping down to the local supermarket, picking up some shrink-wrapped fillet that was caught halfway around the world and scanning my contactless bank card at the checkout. I think that's exactly it: contactless payment for a contactless product in my contactless life. I don't want a contactless life.

M For me, travel is primarily about understanding other people and their cultures. This could be construed as me educating myself, but really I am fundamentally nosy. I have an insatiable curiosity about human beings and how they live their lives, and I believe there is no substitute for experiencing these things for yourself. I know holidays satisfy that need for many, but there is no substitute for engaging in the longer term, living life as a local and getting to know people as neighbours. Now, not everybody has this chance, but living and travelling on a sailboat does offer this unique opportunity.

I am of the firm belief that as human beings, our commonalities far outweigh our differences. It is interesting that as we have evolved, we tend to highlight our differences more than our similarities. I think travel allows us to meet people as equals and to form opinions based on our personal experiences rather than have others mediate that experience for us. One of my favourite quotes of all time comes from the American author Mark Twain: 'Travel is fatal to prejudice, bigotry and narrow-mindedness. Broad wholesome charitable views of men and things cannot be acquired by vegetating in one little corner of the earth all of one's lifetime.' I do not believe for one moment that a person will automatically be less inclined to bigotry, prejudice or narrow mindedness if they travel, no more than I believe living in one place your whole life makes you all of the above. However, travelling can certainly open you up to a whole world of appreciation for the ways in which others live.

Both Leonard and I share a conviction that if you dream it, you can do it. We are bright people and we can find a way to solve whatever problems emerge; we have done it all our adult lives for other people and now it was our time to use those same skills for our own benefit, to follow our dream. Of course, there is the dawning realisation as a mother of teens that Ella and Luke are at a crucial time in their development and I want to influence that development rather than leaving it to technology and social media. I want to provide them with an environment of openness and possibility, and a breadth of experience that will allow them to develop as thoughtful young people who have a positive influence on the society in which they live. It is my wish to equip them with as much insight and experience as I can while I still have that time available to me.

So why did we choose to live on board a sailboat instead of immigrating to another country, the way hundreds of thousands of other people before us have done? There are a few answers for that question. First, I believe when people emigrate from one country to another it is usually for employment offers or opportunities, in addition to the belief that they can achieve a better life for themselves and their families. This is not primarily our motivation; we have had plenty of employment opportunities in Ireland and we are well educated with a very full range of work experience behind us. With regard to employment we would prefer to do short-term jobs while we live on board if we need to earn money. So, our primary reason for choosing water over land has to do with seeking an alternative lifestyle – in other words, using our time creatively for education, experience and broadening our horizons.

Second, a sailboat is quite simply the cheapest and easiest way of living and transporting ourselves and all our goods and chattels. It is not only an effective way of travelling from country to country, but it allows us to rely on our own skill and expertise to do so. I know it is not without risk but with knowledge and planning we can minimise the risk considerably. We are also aware that thousands of people have done it before us and we take our inspiration from them.

So the 'why' for me is simple really – I can, that's why, and we can do it with the resources we have without too much strain and with the effort of our own work and planning. There is something incredibly freeing about taking control of and responsibility for one's own life journey.

3

How much will it cost?

There is a common perception that only the wealthy sail. That if you own a yacht, clearly you are a millionaire. To be honest, I feel uncomfortable referring to *Faoin Spéir* as a yacht, even though that's exactly what she is. I prefer the term 'sailboat'. And I would argue that sailing can be for anyone. A good friend of mine recently (in 2017) sold an Enterprise sailing dinghy, complete with sails, rigging and trailer for just £50. So here we are – for the price of a cheap car tyre, we can be out sailing and enjoying the water. No mooring fees, no marina fees, just tow the boat to the sea or a lake and launch it. It's not the sort of boat that I would like to take into the open ocean, or even around a headland (although many have), but it operates just like its grown-up relations. For the adventurous among us, you could even put a tent over the boom and sleep at anchor in some sheltered hideaway.

At the other end of the scale are the very sleek, very shiny modern yachts that start at a couple of hundred thousand and go as high as you can imagine. I once saw a charter yacht for rent at a cost of £600,000 per week!

Clearly, there is a place on the spectrum of ownership for everyone.

When people ask about *Faoin Spéir*, this is what we tell them: 'She's a 39-foot American boat with three bedrooms and a reasonable living space, kitchen and bathroom.' This would be the general description if we were chatting to people who don't sail, and it all sounds very posh and expensive. In truth, *Faoin Spéir* is an old boat, and she's sailed in the Pacific, the Caribbean and crossed the North Atlantic. She doesn't look like a modern production boat, and in the age of 'bling is best', the door was left open for us to afford a genuine blue water cruiser on a tiny budget.

OK, so maybe you want some hard figures. If budget were not a consideration, the cost of recreational sailing (at time of writing in 2018) might look something like this:

- A second-hand, 30-foot sailboat that would take you comfortably across the English Channel, fully equipped and ready to go: £25,000
- Sail training (shore and practical to Day Skipper level, and marine VHF radio training and certification): £1,500 per person (only one certified person is required on a boat)
- Marina berth for said boat: £2,000 per year
- Lift, antifoul paint (for underwater hulls) and general maintenance: £1,500 per year
- Miscellaneous (fuel, visitor fees, harbour dues etc): £1,000

After the initial purchase of a modest but modern and comfortable yacht, and the training to use it, the running costs come to the bare bones of £100 per week. Now for most of us, this is a nice chunk out of our pay packet. But don't give up hope, for it need not be this expensive.

There are bargains out there. It is possible to buy a 30-foot boat that needs some TLC for a couple of thousand pounds. I personally know of a 32-footer that went complete for just £1,000. However, that took a lot of work to make seaworthy and there's a limit to what even I would take on. So you take your two-grand boat, and you can keep it on a swinging mooring for another few hundred. Sail more, motor less and learn to do your own repairs. Before you know it, your running costs could be as little as £10 per week.

How do recreational sailing and liveaboard cruising compare budget-wise?

Chances are that with liveaboard cruising you will want more boat, and with more boat comes the added expense of more antifoul, thicker ropes, bigger fenders to prevent damage to the sides of your boat, etc. Essentially, the more you use the boat, the greater the maintenance costs. But if we look at the recreational sailor, the maintenance costs may be less, but she also has to keep a house or apartment. So while the cost of running your boat may go up as a liveaboard, you can write off the costs of keeping a domestic property. No more electricity or home heating bills. Of course, when you live on board you have the option of living at anchor rather than on a mooring or in a marina, thus reducing the costs even further.

Now for the big saving: the car. As a liveaboard cruiser, there is little point in owning a car if you spend most of your time away from it. Imagine cutting out the cost of petrol, car tax, insurance, servicing and all other motoring expenses. How much would you save? Do you have a car loan? What do you spend on petrol or diesel each week? How often do you need new tyres? I would be very surprised if the cost of owning and running a car comes to any less than £100 per week.

In rather vague terms, it could be said that the cost of getting to the sail-away stage is 'whatever you have', but in the interest of clarity, here are the hard facts on the *Faoin Spéir* project. Our budget was not a fixed amount. Broadly speaking, if there was no other way forwards than to spend £30,000 on a boat, we would have focused on raising that money. Fortunately, as you will read later, it's not necessary to spend that much. So, our budget was in fact 'whatever it was going to take' to see the project through.

There is one huge question that needs to be answered before looking at your own personal way forwards: are you going for good? If you are planning on simply taking a year out, not only do you need to organise the project but you also have to make sure you have a life to come back to. Do you need to apply for a career break or find (and likely pay for) storage for your furniture? Is there any point in selling everything that won't fit on the boat if you will be back in a year? If you compare this with going for good it can certainly make decision making easier. We jumped in without the intention of returning. If it didn't fit on the boat, there was no point in owning it. I sold my car, my van, my motorbike, anything that was not coming with me. Things that I couldn't sell, I gave away and things that I couldn't give away, I dumped. We focused solely on a budget that would enable us to sail away for good.

Initial costs

The boat and transport

The cost of our sail-away boat was £4,350. This was the single largest necessary cost to the project. After that, the next largest single necessary cost was transport. As we opted to bring the boat to the house rather than pay storage for the two years and nine months it would stand leaning against the shed, we had to swallow some hefty transport and crainage costs. Moving the boat to the garden from the previous owner's yard and having it craned off the trailer came to £600. To many boatowners, this may seem like a bargain, and yes, it was, but at a time when we had just emptied our accounts of £4,350 that £600 seemed like an impossible figure to come up with. However, every now and then – and in fact throughout the entire project – just when the hurdles seemed too high, someone would step in or something would turn up that would make it all possible. On this occasion, it was my brother, John, who by way of a boat-warming gift offered to cover the cost of the crane.

Having the boat in the garden did save a lot on storage and even more on fuel, had we had to drive the 90 minutes to the nearest boatyard, but it did increase the cost of hauling back to the sea when that time came. So, almost three years later, we had to pay £1,400 to get the boat to the water. This included a crane at both ends and a truck with the largest boat trailer available in Ireland at the time. In total, then, the cost of transporting *Faoin Spéir* came to £2,000. Half the price of the boat itself.

The real difficulty with the cost of transport and cranes is that as much as I wracked my brain, I could find no other alternative other than to pay the professionals. Now, they were open to negotiating a good price, and us being flexible with our dates, which allowed them to slot us into a space in their schedule that suited them, helped to make it more affordable, but it still accounted for the biggest cost aside from the boat itself.

Materials

After we had made the purchase and moved the boat into position, we had to start the refit. During this period, time was our best money saver. If you have the patience to wait and the desire to locate them, materials such as hardwoods and fittings can be found for free from building renovation projects. This is where spreading the word of your plans can pay off, with generous offers of old kitchens, church pews and school desks. Even our table was once a teak shed door. This approach meant that the cost of wood was reduced to plywood sheeting where hardwoods would not have worked. Add to this sealant (don't skimp on this), GRP (glass-reinforced plastic, or fibreglass) materials and paint for the deck, topsides, and interior plus antifoul for the hull, and materials ran to about £1,200.

The boat itself, although a stripped-out project, came with all standing and running rigging except for a forestay, three baggy but functional sails and a host of extras, including a liferaft, Navtex (the primary method of receiving marine safety information, or MSI), an anchor and even windvane steering. There were items we opted to replace with more up-to-date versions, like the VHF radio, but all in all I would say that we equipped the boat with change out of £1,700. For this, we bought an EPIRB (or emergency position-indicating radio beacon, a tracking transmitter that is triggered during an incident), a cooker, a sink, water tanks, radios (fitted and hand-held), an AIS (automatic identification system) transponder, an antenna, solar panels and batteries. The costs add up very quickly but, as previously mentioned, this was spread out over four years. We did manage a lot of savings by making second-hand purchases where we could. For example, I bought the EPIRB for £80 from eBay, saving over £350 on a new one. And then I learned to service it myself. The sink was on special offer from a chain hardware store for only £45 and we bought our £700 cooker second-hand from eBay. Again, having time and spreading the

Our sink is a domestic sink, which we bought on special offer
from a chain hardware store.

costs over said time allows you to find the right gear for
the right price.

The water tanks were the one thing that I could not
manage to find on the second-hand market. I spent three
years searching and it came right down to the wire. The
week before we set off from Bere Island, we bought new
tanks from our long-suffering chandler, who gave us a cut
price as a parting gift. These we paid for out of funds from
another parting gift.

So at this stage we had spent around £9,250 getting to
a place where we had our sail-away boat not quite finished
but ready and able to take us anywhere in the world we
wanted.

Certification

Now all we had to do was get ourselves ready to crew. Training for me, of any kind, has always been a contentious issue. Unlike hauling a heavy displacement blue water sailboat halfway across the country, there is much flexibility in how we learn to manage a boat. We cover this elsewhere in the book, so I'll not dwell on it here, but suffice it to say that no country that I know of requires any formal training to skipper a recreational sailboat, but many do require certification. In my research, I have found that we needed five pieces of paper to successfully sail with relative ease around EU countries:

1. Registration papers
2. Insurance
3. One crew member holding an International Certificate of Competency (ICC)
4. Ships Radio Licence (SRL)
5. One crew member holding a VHF Radio Operators Certificate

1. Registration

The costs of and procedures for registration of recreational craft varies from country to country. In the UK, the small ships register fills the roll and so you will often see British boats sporting their SSR numbers on their superstructure. In Ireland, it is an altogether more complex affair. Prior to 2018, there was no special register for leisure craft in the country and so the official procedure for a 20-foot weekend trailer sailor was the very same as that for a 250,000-ton super tanker. For the most part, this wasn't a big deal, as registration of leisure craft is not a requirement in Ireland. But what if you wish to sail under the Irish flag to foreign ports? Then you will need some sort of official registration papers. Rather than going through the convoluted and expensive 'super tanker' registration process for *Faoin Spéir*, I opted to register her with Waterways Ireland, the governmental body responsible for overseeing Ireland's excellent inland waterways system. This was free and painless and allowed us to duly receive a government document identifying Mary and I as owners of *Faoin Spéir*, complete with a record of identifying marks and the all-important registration number. Plans are in place to update the current status in Ireland and create a sort of small ships register by 2018. Watch this space.

2. Insurance

There are many fine insurance companies out there who are happy to go over your needs, so I'll not go into any great detail here. In Ireland, leisure craft do not require insurance, but as it is a requirement in many of the countries that we planned to visit, we never had the conversation as to whether or not to insure; rather, we discussed whether to insure fully comprehensive or third party. It was a choice between £400 or £200 respectively. We thought long and hard about it, and I have to say that my preference was for the cheaper option. However, Mary, whose anxiety was high enough at the prospect of setting out to sea without suggesting that we not be 'fully covered', made the louder argument and so we reached a compromise. We would insure fully for the first year and consider reducing the cover after that. After all, if something was going to go wrong, it was likely to happen when we were still a little green. Fortunately, we have never had to deal with the insurance company beyond paying the premium.

3. International Certificate of Competency (ICC)

The usual route for sailors in Britain and Ireland to obtain the ICC is to complete the five-day Royal Yachting Association (RYA) or Irish Sailing Association (ISA) Day Skipper course, after which you can submit your certification and fee of £45 to the relevant national authority to receive your certificate. The typical cost for the Day Skipper course is around £600 at the time of writing (2018). The cost of completing a two-day ICC assessment was £230. I opted for the latter, since what we really needed was an ICC, and whether I had 20 years' transatlantic sailing under my belt or a two-day assessment, the officials only wanted to see an ICC with my photo on it. The total cost of our assessment and certification was therefore £275.

4. and 5. Ships Radio Licence and VHF Radio Operators Certificate

We are not required by law to carry a radio but from a safety point of view, I wouldn't like to go to sea without one. This meant that we needed two things: a Ships Radio

Licence and a qualified operator. As I had completed the ICC, Mary volunteered to take on the VHF Radio Operators' course. It is possible to sit the exam without completing the course, but as Mary had no previous experience with radio communication, we felt it would be of greater benefit to complete the two-day course and exam all in one go. This came to £250, after which we could apply for the Ships Radio Licence for £85. So the total cost of radio compliance for our VHF radios, AIS and EPIRB came to £325 if we throw in lunch.

Overall, to put ourselves in a position where we can enter most countries in the world and certainly all of those in the European Union, we spent £1,000. We could have cut those costs had we needed to by settling for third party-only insurance and doing the VHF exam rather than the course but we felt that this was the right way to go for us.

By the time we had both *Faoin Spéir* and ourselves sufficiently equipped, we had just approached ten grand and we were certified, with a boat in the water and ready to go. Spread over four years, it breaks down to less than £50 per week. At the time of writing, £10,000 will buy you a six-year-old Volkswagen Golf in reasonable condition.

Ongoing costs

For many of those whom we chat to about our cruising lifestyle, the subject of money and cost is never far away. We've covered in great depth how we got to the stage of owning a liveaboard blue water cruising boat and setting off on our journey, but sustaining it is a whole other ball game. Before going any further, I'll give you the short answer: in 2017, our typical spend on a liveaboard for a family of four was £85 per week. In reality, with so many variables this really doesn't mean anything to anyone but ourselves.

We didn't have a big stash of money before getting the boat ready and in the water, and ourselves on board and underway, and nothing has changed. So, our week-to-week life tends to be on a budget. Every liveaboard cruiser that we have met along the way is in the same position. Even those who have great wealth or giant pensions behind them when they set out are watching their budget. If you are in it for the long term, like for the rest of your life, then there is a tendency to mind your spending. Of course I have met those for whom it is a three-year trip, and they have saved very hard before setting out in the knowledge that they wish to have X amount per month for their luxury whizz around the world. They enjoy every minute of it right up until they return to land and work and traffic jams and all of those other things that most long-term liveaboard cruisers are escaping.

So, how much do I need per week to be a liveaboard cruiser? That is how most people phrase the question, and I was one of those people. Before setting out, I started to develop an obsession with a weekly budget that would sustain our life on board, and how we could generate that money as we travelled. What I found in practice was that the question needed to be rephrased to 'What can I do to reduce the costs of living aboard?'

First, the obvious things – cooking on board and shopping conservatively. If the choice is between having a full English breakfast every day of your three-month cruise or porridge, boiled eggs and fruit every day of your 12-month cruise, I know which one I'd choose. I'm not simply pulling this out of the air; a bowl of porridge, a boiled egg and a banana will cost you less than £1 a day, and what a great start to the day. By contrast, you'd be hard pushed to prepare a full English breakfast for less than £4, and you'll pay twice that if you eat out. So it's not about how much it costs to live aboard, it's more about how much you can *save*. It's pretty straightforward: cooking on board means you can stay cruising at least four times longer than if you eat out all the time. The same goes for drinks and entertainment: the more self-sufficient you are around these things, the longer you can cruise on the same money and, in our experience, the more fun you will have. Without question, we've had some of our best times when we've had friends round for dinner or cooked at their place.

In truth, everyone will give you a different answer for budgeting living expenses, and from what I can tell, the most accurate answer is that you will spend what you can. If your cruising coffers are on the healthy side, you may choose to pull into a nice marina close to the city centre, so you can enjoy all the luxuries it has to offer. Occasionally we do this. When things are a little tight, you can anchor off and enjoy the wild freedom that comes with swinging with the tide and wind. Most cruisers we know live like this. Becky and Éamonn from Cork live aboard *Wayward*. Over around three months, they cruised from Ireland, took a coastal route along the west of France, northern Spain and down to the south of Portugal. They spent only two nights in marinas, preferring to anchor off.

Living and cruising on a boat is really no different to living on land when it comes to budgeting. Too many would-be cruisers stay at home for fear of the unexpected. But the unexpected pops up all the time on land and we deal with it. When you have a little more in the bank, you might treat yourself to dinner out, when you have a sudden unexpected expense that leaves you short, the world doesn't suddenly end, you get by. The same can be said for living on a boat. At the extreme end of the scale, I could conceive of a single person cruising aboard a well-managed boat of about 30 feet getting by on £20 per week, but I wouldn't want to do that for too long (there's only so much pasta, rice and baked beans one can eat). If you prefer to spend most of your nights in a marina, and eat out at a reasonably priced establishment once a week but usually cook for yourself, then £300 per week will allow you some comfort. Most of us operate somewhere in between.

Generating income

Although we can begin to afford our lifestyle by cutting costs, it is a fact of life that some income must be generated in addition. This can range from the traditional 'looking for work where you find it' to maintaining your stock market interests, from writing to producing online content. Let's weigh up some of the options.

Laptop office

The digital world is your oyster. With the ubiquitous availability of internet connection these days, there is ample opportunity to work remotely. I'm not saying that you need to move your old office job to your new life as a liveaboard. Cost cutting means the need to earn less, so perhaps you can continue doing what you've always done but on a part-time or freelance basis. We know one accountant turned liveaboard who wrapped up her business to escape under sail. Before winding down, she identified a handful of low-maintenance clients that needed minor tending to and kept them on remotely. This generates enough to keep her afloat and cruising.

There are many professions that could work this way. Essentially, anything that requires the exchange of digital files and a laptop, such as a wage clerk, exam tutor, video editor, proofreader – the list goes on. We fall under this 'laptop office' heading via our writing. Obviously the book that you are reading (and hopefully enjoying) is an example of this work. Combined with occasional magazine articles and other writing projects, we can stay fed. It may not make us rich, but we don't need to be rich.

Video blogging (vlogging) is a fairly recent development in the world of remote income, and it has proven very successful for some sailors, but for us resulted in generating about £500 per year. Not to be sniffed at, as that sort of money goes a long way on board, but for the amount of time required to produce the sort of quality viewing that people have come to expect from vlogs, we found our efforts were best focused elsewhere.

Old-fashioned graft

If you are the outgoing sort, then there is always work to be found on the move, whether it's tending bar for the high season in a beach resort or washing dishes for a couple of weeks of holiday cover in a local restaurant. Some care and common sense must be exercised when taking this route. Are you legally allowed to work in the country? There is a great advantage to being in the European Union – at least for now, in the case of the UK – and being free to travel and work in any of the 26 member countries and their respective islands dotted across the globe. However, this does not extend to other countries. Were we, as Irish citizens, to so much as wipe a glass in the USA, we could soon find ourselves answering some awkward questions in an emigration office. Even if you can legally work in a country, do consider if you may be stepping on some local toes before seeking work. It could be that a local usually provides the holiday cover for the dishwasher mentioned above. Wherever you go, you will be a guest and visitor, for a while at least, so do remember to behave like one.

I have found one job that we can rely on to be available and welcomed in most ports: playing music. Although one has to be careful, as above, not to step on local toes, it's my experience that the local musicians are the very ones encouraging passing musicians to play.

Never too far from Leonard's hands. We carry about ten different instruments on board, from whistles to guitars.

If your skills extend to sewing, diving or engineering (in particular electrical, electronic or mechanical), we've found that if you follow the popular cruising grounds, you will never be too far from regular casual work.

Ⓜ I think everybody has a unique relationship with money and we all develop that over a lifetime. How we spend it and earn it is shaped by how important it is to us. There is often huge shame attached to money and how we use it. For example, one of the worst insults you could say to an Irish person is that they are 'tight' with money, meaning they are mean and will not spend it, especially with others. But what if a person has very little money and cannot afford to spend it? A good example is presents at work. Different workplaces have different traditions, but in staffrooms, for example, it is usual to buy a wedding present for a colleague who is getting married. Now everybody loves to acknowledge the blossoming of a new relationship and celebrate that significant step. But what if that collection comes in the middle of the pay cycle, when your rent or mortgage and car insurance have gone out of your account and you're already in deficit? Taking a tenner out to contribute to a gift will incur a penalty in interest, so where does that leave you?

Another factor in the gift-giving scenario is not everybody in the workplace has the same earning capacity. Your newly appointed part-time worker is not earning as much as somebody who has been on staff for ten years in a permanent position and therefore cannot contribute the same amount. But conversations about money embarrass us or make us feel vulnerable or tip into a deep well of shame, so these conversations do not usually take place.

However, in order to plan for an eventuality like cruising, there has to be full and frank disclosure about finances and how they will be used for the benefit of all concerned. It is essential; there is no other way.

4

Choosing a boat

M Honestly, when we started our search for a boat I had no notion of what we were looking for. I would leaf through magazines or view boats online, and all I could see was how pretty they were. But I started reading and I tormented Leonard with questions, and before I knew it I had learned a little.

My first experience of sailing was in our 24-foot Achilles. I had mixed feelings about that boat. I loved that she had a tiller through which I could feel the impact of the wind in the sails and adjust what I was doing accordingly. I loved how in tight spaces we could move her with a deeply reefed mainsail or just a paddle. I was not too impressed by the aft cockpit, as we regularly got quite wet on the lake and when we heeled it looked like we were going to be tossed promptly into the water. I was tormented by the position of the forward hatch; it was over the 'V' berth, where Leonard and I slept. It had a worn seal so when it rained – and in Ireland it rains perpetually – there was a drip right on my head! There was no room to move, so we commonly slept holding a basin over our heads to collect the drips, or at least Leonard did! Another good thing about owning the Achilles was that by the time we were buying *Faoin Spéir* I had moved beyond the glossy image of sailboats to realising they were functional and not just pretty little things.

I knew nothing about keels, or what they did, or their importance to sailing. Now I am very content to be sailing a boat in the open sea with an encapsulated keel. My technical knowledge is limited and I worry about a container or another boat hitting our *plastic* boat, although I now know that our plastic boat is sturdier than many modern vessels due to the tendency of boatyards to 'overbuild' early fibreglass models.

I got fussy, too. I did not want, and would never want, a catamaran, and I apologise in advance to catamaran owners, and I know there are pros and cons to living aboard one, but they frighten the living daylights out of me. I was watching the YouTube channel Sailing La Vagabonde, which is run by Riley and Elayna, a young Australian couple. In one video they give viewers a tour of their new catamaran. I had to stop after 10 minutes, as my anxiety levels were through the roof.

I've often looked at sailboats on the outside and thought, 'Gosh, aren't they tiny; how do people live on them?' Now I know that what you see when you look at a boat on the water is probably the smallest part of the boat. They are far more spacious than they seem.

Since I started living on *Faoin Spéir* I have visited many boats and I love seeing the layouts of other vessels. Space is at a premium, and so it is used with great care.

We designed our living space from scratch to suit ourselves and our needs. The maximum amount of space goes to the salon and galley, the living room and kitchen respectively – rooms that are used by everybody. Ours is a tiny space compared to most houses but it is huge compared with most boats. I often sit and look around, thinking 'This is luxury', but I lived in a tiny house before I moved on board so the adjustment was not so huge for me.

Leonard says most boats are a compromise. I think we were lucky to find *Faoin Spéir*. She is a fine, solid boat with a centre cockpit. I look at boats with aft cockpits and feel envious that they can berth stern-to and step off so easily, but I know that at sea I would be terrified to be in an aft cockpit; the sea would be much too close. I love that the aft cabin, where Leonard and I sleep, has privacy and we can access it without having to go outside the boat. I love that we have desks where we can sit and work, and space for bookshelves, more so than any boat I have visited thus far.

Now you're probably reading this and thinking 'So what?', but that is the point: what is right for us would not work for you and what is right for you would not work for us. You have to figure out what is right to help you to achieve your own dreams.

What do you want from a boat?

Before you can consider what boat to buy, you'll need to answer some very basic questions about what exactly it is you want from a boat. I know this might seem like an obvious and silly point, but consider this: perhaps you have a highly stressful job with lots of responsibility and you are very highly paid for your time but you are full-on for 55 hours a week. When you sail at the weekend, you want a luxurious yacht that has ice on tap so you can have a cool gin and tonic and sit back with your husband and enjoy your alone time. You want comfort, cleanliness and to be well looked after with all mod cons. You want to get to your destination quickly with minimum fuss. You do not want a project boat, or to waste your time with your husband, with him stuck in some bolt hole, drilling and glassing and doing god knows what else – after all, there is DIY and then there is boat DIY!

If you are considering taking your boat to the Mediterranean for a summer cruise or berthing it there for winter to use for cruising in summer with friends or family or grown-up children, then you are looking for a different kind of boat again, and your budget might be akin to buying a summer residence. You will have different criteria, different things that are important to you.

Therefore, my advice is to be as clear as possible about what it is you want from a boat, where you are planning to use it and in what type of weather primarily. Once you're sure you know, you can begin your search.

If you have made the decision to uproot your family to live aboard a boat and travel for the foreseeable future, then you have an entirely different set of considerations. What kind of life do you want to lead and what kind of boat can you afford to suit this life? In my opinion the only thing you have in common with the previous examples is that you want to buy a boat – we are talking apples and oranges. A simple question like 'How long do you plan to live on board and cruise?' becomes a major consideration. For example, if you are the parents of two small children and want to cruise for a year, the kind of boat you need is very different from the same parents with the same kids who are planning to cruise indefinitely.

Points to consider before buying a boat

Before you start looking for a boat you should think about the following:

- Do you have an idea of how long you would like to live on board and cruise?
- Are you both able to sail a boat?
- Do you have children? If so, what are their ages?
- What needs do your children have? How does this affect space, safety, comfort, entertainment, education, development and equipment?
- How will you divide the sailing, parenting, cooking, passage planning, DIY, boat maintenance and education?
- How will you support yourselves financially?
- How resilient/tough does your boat need to be?
- What kind of access does your boat need to have for you and your kids and their equipment? Do they have a buggy or bike, for example?

- How will you manage to get time to yourselves/ privacy?
- Do you need room for guests?
- Will you do night passages? If so, who will tend to the young children while night sailing?

There are probably a number of additional issues relevant to you that I have not considered, but these are a good starting point.

Hull material

The technical specification of a production boat is particular to the model you choose, and the technical specification is relevant. However, it must fit in with your family circumstances first and foremost. One of the few things that we can say for certain is that there is no such thing as the perfect boat. All boats are a compromise. Although modern sailboats are mostly made from glass reinforced plastic (GRP, or fibreglass) there are many hull materials to choose from. Each has its own advantages and disadvantages, and none should be discounted without due consideration.

For the purposes of this book, we're going to cover the more common hull materials and leave the specialist materials to those sailors who know more than we do. I've already mentioned the most popular, which is GRP. It really is a marvellous material, since it can be moulded into almost any shape, is flexible, watertight and long lasting, with very little maintenance required. However, all these positives pale into insignificance compared to the benefits to manufacturers. With a mould, a manufacturer can turn out hull after hull in a fraction of the time that a wooden boat of the same size and shape would take. And all this without the need for the sort of skills honed over decades of wooden boatbuilding. The disadvantage is that GRP is not as strong as steel, aluminium or even a wooden plank-built boat. But there is that compromise again.

Steel is obviously the strongest of the common materials, but it requires much more maintenance due to the aversion steel has to sea water. Aluminium is seen by many as the ideal but it too can fall foul of corrosion.

Ferro-cement is an interesting material, and many have sailed the world in boats constructed using wire mesh and mortar. There are always great bargains to be had in the line of ferro-cement boats, and this should be a warning. There are very few such boats around in boatyards. The vast majority are home-built projects and so there can be a broad spectrum of quality. GRP boats have been sold as kit boats but the hull has generally been constructed in a professional boatyard, meaning that one should expect adherence to certain standards. So how do you go about buying a ferro-cement boat? The same way as you go about buying any boat: carefully.

Although wood has been seen as the traditional, old-fashioned boatbuilding material it is making a comeback – not in the same format, however. We have gone from planks on ribs via plywood sheets and fibreglass joints to cold-moulded wooden hulls.

This last evolution of wooden boatbuilding has a lot going for it. With cold-moulded wooden hulls you get the beautiful smooth lines that are so easily achieved with GRP, but with a stronger material that provides better natural insulative properties and so less condensation.

Plywood, like ferro-cement, has been very popular with amateur boatbuilders. Take care not to take the word 'amateur' to mean low quality or rubbish; there are many excellent examples of amateur-built boats that have circumnavigated the globe and are still sailing through conditions that would challenge many professionally built boats. But, again, you must be careful. Plywood has this habit of rotting below the waterline in the most inaccessible places. I personally have never bought a boat that I've not seen out of the water. It just happened that way, and while I would consider buying a GRP boat without a haul out, I would always need to check a plywood boat from the underside.

Size

In sailing, size does help. Sure, you can sail from Britain to New Zealand in an Achilles 24, along with your partner, a Great Dane, two kittens and a budgie, but who'd want to? This question of size relates directly to your needs. I personally would not fancy the prospect of crossing the Atlantic Ocean in anything smaller than a 30-foot, well-found sailboat. So if that is part of the plan, this should be the lower end of your scale. Equally, there is not much point in a solo sailor trying to run a 60-foot boat that has not been modified for solo sailing. According to most reading that I've done, and the long-term cruisers that I've met, generally the 36- to 46-foot bracket suits most couples as a compromise in comfort versus manoeuvrability, not forgetting the marina charges if you decide to treat yourself. A concrete example of this is Cork City, on the south coast of Ireland. The last time we visited, there was a nightly charge of £17 per night for boats up to 12 metres

Tying up right in the centre of a city is something
every cruising sailor should try.

long, whereas boats over 12 metres incurred a charge of £30. So there was a 75 per cent increase in cost per night from a 39 footer to a 40 footer!

A typical boat of around 40 foot will have three cabins, and so is perfectly workable for a family of four. As there were to be four of us on board our boat, our preferred deck layout was a centre cockpit. This permitted an aft cabin of reasonable size, giving a little more privacy and distance between the living space and us. A centre cockpit also tends to feel less exposed at sea and, as such, is less scary for a crew with fewer sea miles under their belt.

The difficulty with a centre cockpit is that it can make mooring stern-to quite tricky, and fishing while sailing is a bit of a nuisance. The real concern with a centre cockpit is taking a wave. Unlike many modern aft cockpit boats that have at least part of the transom open, the centre cockpit can take quite a while to drain. The disadvantages of a centre cockpit are many, but for us the accommodation and comfort in a seaway trumps all.

The keel

Ah yes, now this is an interesting one, and if you search online for 'What sort of keel should my boat have?' you will turn up all sorts of debates in the forums, some of which can become quite nasty, such is the strength of feeling. Here are some hard facts about keel designs that might help you choose your preferred design:

- A long keel generally has the best defence against leeway but is less manoeuvrable than a fin keel (particularly in reverse).
- A deep fin keel generates less friction through the water and so is quicker, but it is more vulnerable to getting caught in submerged ropes and cables, like those from nets and pots.
- Bilge keels are great for taking the ground and sailing in shallow waters, like those in the south-east of England, but they are slower and demonstrate less stability than their fin and long-keel incarnations.
- Lifting keels can be a great compromise, giving the best of both shallow capabilities and deep fin stability, or if badly designed you may end up with a boat that does neither very well.

One debate that shows up time and again is that of the bolt-on versus encapsulated keel. In fact, I was looking for a bolt-on but found an encapsulated keel boat that had everything else going for it. My desire for the bolt-on keel was driven by my fear of grounding; I would prefer to have a large lump of steel hitting the bottom than a layer of GRP. It's fine if said bottom is made of sand or mud, but if it's a rocky, there is a real fear that some damage might be done, resulting in an expensive haul-out and repair job. On the other hand, there have been some scary stories about occasions where the keels have literally fallen off the boat to which they were bolted, in some cases resulting in the tragic loss of life.

For me, each of the keels I mention above has a long history and healthy track record. None is perfect, but all have crossed oceans successfully. So to my mind, the shape or structure of your keel is less important than your ability to manage its shortcomings and exploit its advantages.

The rig

The same could be said for the rig. With so many layouts to choose from, every sailor has their own preference. I had hoped to find a ketch. I figured if by some chance in the future we were unfortunate enough to be dismasted, we would always have a second mast to get us home. But what about all of that extra rigging, both standing and running? Extra sails to stow and handle? Friends of ours on *Wayward* took the rig question very seriously and went for a junk rig – minimal running rigging, no standing rigging and to top it all off they put up two masts, so if one failed they always had another.

So why are all sailboats not junk rigged? Just like keels and deck layouts, each style has its advantages and disadvantages. The junk rig does not sail into the wind as efficiently as does the classic Bermudian rig. Having completed several thousand miles as a liveaboard cruiser, I have changed my persuasion and have aligned myself with Hal Roth, who prefers the Bermudian rig for its ease of handling on a shorthanded boat and the flexibility of direction relative to the wind.

But again, the various popular designs have all proven themselves to be ocean crossers and I would say that they are all worth considering when shopping for your sail-away boat. I'd rather be sailing the South Pacific islands on a junk rigged bilge keeler than sitting in a flat in Gravesend, waiting for the right boat to turn up.

5

Buying a boat

The biggest part of the puzzle in our journey to escape under sail was obviously the vessel. We needed a boat, and it had to be affordable. Initially I had looked around the various 'boats for sale'-type websites, and I figured that the best that we could reasonably hope for was to find a 40-foot blue water boat that needed a lot of work for about £25,000. This was well beyond our budget, but if this was the best we could do, we would simply have to figure out a way to raise the funds. I searched all over Europe via the internet. Depending on the condition, if the right boat showed up in France, Spain or even Greece, we could always sail it back to Ireland and work on it there. It was here that the search took the sort of coincidental twist of fate that is usually reserved for fiction.

My brother, John, had recently bought a boat for use on Lough Derg, and we'd been chatting on the phone about various ideas to refit its ageing and tired interior. The model happened to be a 'Project 31' from the 1970s. After hanging up the phone, I decided to do a little research online to see what others had done with the same model. I went to the boat section of a popular classified ads website and typed a single word into the search bar: 'Project'. It seems obvious now that it would list *all* the 'project' boats alongside examples of the 'Project 31'. And there it was before me: 'Project yacht for sale – Yorktown 39'. It was less than a half hour from us. After searching the length and breadth of Europe, our sail-away boat was just a few miles away sitting on a trailer. The asking price was €10,600 (£9,200), and a project boat it most certainly was. I dialled the number on the screen and spoke to the owner, John Sinnott, a most likable man whom we have since found to be generous with his advice, time and, when called upon to move masts, booms and sails, his muscle power. I remember suggesting to him that although the price was very fair, I didn't actually have the money but would love to pop over for a look. He was happy to oblige. Now, at this stage we really did not have the money, and I fully expected to go there, have a look around and have a chat with a very experienced sailor about our plans before coming away with a little more knowledge, but still without a boat.

I phoned my brother and asked if he'd be up for a nose around an old Yorktown 39, and he drove an hour to meet me there. John, an experienced sailor and fine furniture maker, had bought the boat several years before with the intention of refitting it in a way that better suited his needs. Having seen examples of John's work, I'm sure the finished product would have been stunning; however, life got in the way, he hadn't got much further than stripping it down and he found himself with one too many boats. This one had to go.

My brother and I climbed the ladder into what could best be described as a construction site. You could run your finger along the fibreglass weave from the transom to the bow. But it was perfect! Well, not perfect, but the perfect compromise. Centre cockpit, Atlantic crossing pedigree, and big enough for a liveaboard family. But at this stage in the project, it was outside our price range. While I saw the perfect boat, my brother's face had 'Are you mad?!' written all over it.

We descended the ladder and I began to tell the owner about our noble plans to fix up an old sailboat and move aboard to sail off to a life less usual. He explained how the bobstay on his Formosa 47 had failed on a recent crossing from France and that he needed the trailer from under the Yorktown 39 sooner rather than later. I reiterated what I had said on the phone, that it was beyond my budget but it seemed to be the closest I would ever come to finding the ideal boat. I wonder if my brother saw what was coming, because he slipped away, and in an apologetic manner I explained that while I couldn't make a reasonable offer, I'd lay all my cards on the table: what we did have was €3000 (£2,670). John smiled and, without offence, said while the money wasn't important, he couldn't in good conscience just give the boat away, *but...* and here it is – the three-letter word that can save an entire project – but, if I could come up to €5000 (£4,450), then 'we'll get you closer to your dream'. Suddenly it felt so close – but I didn't have €5000! My immediate thought was surely if we really put our minds to it, we could come up with the extra €2k. I remembered that I had several outstanding invoices for my tutoring work and offered that I could give him the €3k now if he was OK to wait six weeks for the other €2k. And with that, through John's goodwill and trust, one week later we had our sail-away boat leaning against a shed in the garden.

My brother on our first viewing of 'home'.

Manoeuvring *Faoin Spéir* (then *Pendragon*) after six years
sitting on her trailer.

Boat brokerage

The acquisition of our boat through classified ads is just
one of many approaches. There is a more straightforward
and traditional way, which may also be the most expensive.
Much like buying a car, you go to a place that sells boats,
you look around, kick a few keels, and listen to the
salesman sing the praises of his wares. One key difference
between car sales and boat sales, however, is that it is the
showroom owner or employee of the owner that usually
sells the car. That is to say, you are buying from the garage.
In the case of boat sales, unless you're buying brand new,
it's likely you'll be buying from a private individual

through a third party in the form of a broker. This adds a few complications that can both impede and enhance the buying of a boat.

On the plus side, most boat brokers build their reputation on sound customer service, and will try to be open about the boat's history and condition (although care must be taken nonetheless). Often a brokerage can be a one-stop shop; the broker may have a hundred boats for you to browse through, saving you weeks of driving around the coast following up on listings in the classifieds.

So what's the downside? There are costs tied into the purchase price of boats for sale through a broker. Obviously the brokerage firm has to be paid out of the deal, and let's not forget that the individual salesman must also be paid. So, before the person selling the boat sees their asking price, two other parties must get their cut on top of it. This creates an immediate discrepancy between what the boat is worth to the owner and what the boat is worth to the buyer.

Let's say you do a deal with a boat broker for £10,000. The salesman might get 5 per cent commission on the sale and the brokerage takes another 5 per cent. The boat's owner receives £9,000 – clearly this is a figure he's happy with, otherwise he wouldn't have agreed to it. You, on the other hand, have spent £10,000 on the same boat. We now have two individuals involved at the same time, valuing the boat at £9,000 and £10,000 respectively. Which is right? Who cares; what it really means is that the £10,000 boat you just bought is only worth £9,000 to someone who knows the boat better than you do.

The classifieds

Let's assume that you are in the majority that does buy a boat second-hand, then the alternative to a broker is trawling through the classifieds. In my experience, the more boat-related the publication, the higher the asking price. Most yachting magazines advertise their boats at market price. Of course, market price is simply a spin-off of the typical asking price. (Have you ever sold anything via a classified ad? The first thing you do is check similar ads and base your asking price on what's already available.) This is useful if you're looking to buy with a view to selling on in the future. For example, when you shop for a car, you look at the going rate for your preferred make and model and try to buy for a little under that, often with the knowledge of its value in 12 months' time.

However, if you're reading this book, there's a good chance you're thinking of having your boat for much longer than a year. In fact, I'd hope that you're thinking of keeping the boat for the rest of your long and adventure-filled life. If this is the case, the boat's 'monetary value' disappears the moment you buy it. Therefore, for a blue water liveaboard cruiser, the best value by far can be had from one-off boat sales. In this case, when the seller tries to set a price, there are no others for sale, so a 'market price' does not exist. The seller will then check similar boats from a variety of manufacturers, and the price for a boat with the same specifications tends to vary wildly depending on the brand.

Regardless of how you approach buying your future floating home, time will be your best asset. Many people say that we got a rare bargain with *Faoin Spéir* but the reality was, we were not in a position to buy anything but a bargain. We had four years in which to find our boat and had seen bargains come and go, but when the right one came along, we jumped on it. If we'd had to make a purchase within 12 months, we'd have been forced into spending more on a boat that didn't suit our needs. So take your time. Every day, research what is available. Don't be afraid to send an email or pick up the phone. The seller will be only too happy to hear from you. And be sure to look everywhere; remember that a boat, particularly the type of boat you're looking for, is designed to travel across the ocean. So look in other countries – you can always sail it back. The wider your search, across both time and geography, the greater the chances of finding a boat that ticks all of your boxes at a price that suits your budget.

Like all other aspects of sailing, shopping for the right boat at the right price takes practice. But before you start shopping, you need to know exactly what it is you want from your floating home.

Ten questions to consider when looking for a project boat

There are any number of articles, books and 'how to' videos that guide you through what places to poke and which parts to prod when scrutinising a potential project boat. But before you ever get to crawl around on your belly, or immerse yourself in temperate waters clad in snorkel and mask or pick up the phone to enquire about an ad that optimistically states 'Boat Needs Some Tidying', make sure you sit down with a cup of tea and ponder the following questions.

1. What exactly do I want?

Are you looking for your first boat or simply to move up a couple of feet? Would you like a project as a means of getting more boat for your money, or do you have a long-term plan to work your way through several projects before arriving at the helm of your ultimate boat?

If you're just starting out, there are plenty of small cruisers in the 17- to 20-foot category that are sailing and trailing but need nothing more than basic DIY skills to get passers-by commenting on what a smart little boat you have. My first sailboat was a 17-foot Pirate Express and all she required was cleaning, sanding, oiling and painting throughout. This was the ideal scenario; every weekend, I was learning to both sail *and* work on boats.

If you already have a boat, you can relax and linger over the search for your next project. Take this time to really explore what you want from a boat, where you want to travel, how you plan to use it. If you decide that you ultimately want a 50-foot world cruiser but don't have the budget, your next project should be easily turned around so that you can move on up the marine ladder to your dream boat.

2. What is my budget?

This may seem like an obvious one, but the condition of the boat will determine how much investment is needed to bring it up to standard. If your budget is £5,000, do you find a boat for £1,000 and spend £4,000 on doing it up, or do you find a boat for £4,000 and spend £1,000 on repairs? The answer lies somewhere in between. The biggest factor when it comes to keeping within budget is time. The more time you have, the more you can save on the purchase and restoration. I have often heard it said that the best time to buy something is when you don't need it, and this is especially true of project boats. If you don't need what the seller has for sale, you have a distinct advantage in the negotiations. It also holds true that if you are not in a hurry to complete the project, you can shop around for the best deals on materials and parts etc. Of course, if this is your first boat, you will be eager to get on the water as quickly as possible, in which case you will have to endure the related costs.

3. Where will I store the boat while refitting?

This can be a real problem, especially if the boat doesn't have a trailer. Do you leave it in the water, on hard standing, in storage or bring it home? For smaller boats – up to about 25 feet for fin keelers and a bit longer for the shallower (more trailable) draft boats – I would be looking for one on a trailer so that I could bring it home. This means the boat is always there to remind you just how far behind you are falling. If you have to drive even just 30 minutes to the boat to work on it, you realistically need a spare three hours to make the journey worth your while, whereas if the boat is right outside, there's nothing like popping out for 20 minutes to work on the boat while the dinner's in the oven. You also save on petrol.

Of course, if you are looking at a larger restoration, say of that blue water cruiser, then you have to include specialist transport to get it to your garden. It might well be cheaper to have the boat lifted and stored by the water, and to drive to and fro.

4. Would I prefer to be out sailing?

Some people enjoy slaving over the boat for a year or more, then once they've sailed it for a couple of months they want to move on to the next project. If this is definitely not you, you may be better picking up a boat that needs some TLC rather than a full-blown project boat. Surely a 17-foot weekend cruiser in the water that you can take out anytime is better that the 24-footer in your garden that is turning increasingly mouldy because the enthusiasm for restoration just isn't there.

5. How complete is the boat?

The cost of a mast would soon have you wondering if your project boat was the bargain you thought it was. But the mast is one of those 'hard to miss' things. Consider the cost of each block, pulley or turnbuckle. Even a toddler's shoebox of these parts can run into £1,000 if they're missing. Your boat doesn't have to be in one piece, but it should be complete to the point that if you do get completely fed up, you can always put it back together and sail it, regardless of whether the galley has a gimbal or not.

6. Is it the bargain of a lifetime?

Try to avoid getting carried away. Buying a boat can be a very emotional process, so you'll need to listen to those niggling doubts that crop up; there's nothing as deflating as having misspent your budget on the wrong thing. Besides, while looking for projects I see 'bargains of a lifetime' pop up once every two or three months, so it's not the end of the world if the first one gets away from you. Patience is key.

Remember to weigh up the true value of a 'bargain'. Extras, such as lifejackets, a radio, ropes, an anchor chain, possibly a tender or mooring costs, or even an outboard engine, can greatly add value to a purchase if included.

7. Where do I look?

To get a good deal, you have to be a little more creative than searching local ads. Some of the best deals are to be had from owners who are not actually selling their boat. If we return to the guy who has started his project, but it is now becoming increasingly mouldy in his driveway because he hasn't got either the time or inclination to press on, then maybe it's time to bump into him and ask if he would like to free up that space. Be sure to chat with other boatowners — somebody usually knows where there's a tired old boat slowly sinking on a swinging mooring.

8. Am I just dreaming?

What's wrong with dreaming? Can you round up £100? If you can then you have enough to become a boatowner and get out on the water, for this is all you need to spend on materials to purchase a small dinghy. There are lots of free boat plans online, along with instructional videos on simple boatbuilding techniques. Borrow a jigsaw and with a little ingenuity you'll be underway. OK, so you'll not cross oceans, but if you make a good job of a couple of dinghies, you could quickly find yourself building a small cruiser.

9. What can I do myself?

What do you have at your disposal? Do you have a complete engineering and woodworking workshop? Or are you the proud owner of a rusty bushman saw and an old hammer you found in the garden? Are you a master boatbuilder or do you have six thumbs on each hand? Most of us are somewhere in between. The right tool will certainly make life easier for you, but you have to weigh up the cost.

As for know-how, having the manual skills to complete a restoration is just a matter of putting the time in, asking the right questions and practice. There is nothing about a boat that is conjured from magic; if one set of hands made it in the first place, your hands can learn to fix it or remake it.

10. When is enough, enough?

I have heard of ten-year restoration projects, many of which should have been in the water in year five but they just needed one more scratch polishing out, or were waiting to find a brass traveller in just the right shade of verdigris. This is how many of us wish to treat our project, but if we ever want to actually sail, there comes a time when we have to recognise that boats belong in the water and a sailing boat will always be an ongoing project. It all goes back to the first point: be clear about what it is you want. After a couple of projects, you'll find what works best for you. We all have our own set of boxes to tick before buying, and we all develop our own strategies for completing the project.

What works best for me is to buy a boat that has a sound hull, standing rigging and usable running rigging and sails. Basically, it's a boat I could assemble and sail within a week. This way I always know that if I ever grow tired of the restoration, I can still go sailing. Then I work on the boat, doing all the jobs that are easiest while out of the water (deck joints, rubbing strake, painting the topsides, antifouling, anything 'up the mast' while it's lying flat). The work continues until spring, then regardless of what condition the accommodation is in, I take it on the water. I like to call this the 'Moitessier approach'. Bernard Moitessier always maintained that once you have a boat that can sail, you can always do the rest of the work on the way. As most sailors love the feeling of being on the water, there is a boost to the enjoyment of restoration when you know that you can do a couple of hours' work in the morning, take her out for a sail and continue with a little more work that evening, or even when underway.

6

Hands on

Ⓛ I often talk about boatowners being on a spectrum, from those who can easily afford boats to those who can easily fix them. Most of us fall somewhere between the two in that, generally speaking, if you can sail a boat then you have the ability to manipulate ropes and winches, tie knots and withstand the physicality of being on a boat underway. If you can do all of these things, you are capable of a bit of DIY.

Equally, you must accept that you'll need to spend money on a boat. Mary and I have got where we are on a tiny budget but we couldn't have got here on *no* budget. It's all a balance. If you have a very small budget, many decisions are made for you. The bigger your budget, the more decisions you have to make, although many of these decisions are of course made easier with a bigger budget.

Hiring vs DIY

Every boat – new, old, restored and refitted – needs some work before it can become your liveaboard home. Perhaps it's a total rebuild of the inside as we had to do on *Faoin*

Spéir, or it might be as simple as rebedding some deck fittings and antifouling below the waterline. Whichever it is, you have to decide who will do the work, and where it will be done. Doing things for yourself may not always work out cheaper but may in the long term be worth it.

Let's say you have an iron bolt-on keel and it needs sandblasting. It's not a big job but there are so many variables involved that it can make for some difficult decisions. Do you hire a sandblaster for a couple of days? If so, you track down a place that hires out such equipment, drive to the hire company to collect it, buy the sand and return to the boat. Maybe you have to buy a mask and other protective gear. Then you spend two days sandblasting – poorly at first, because you are new to it – and then at the end of day two you return the gear.

Or, if you happen to be on the hard in a boatyard, or near a mobile sandblasting unit, do you simply get a professional to do it in a few hours for the same price or possibly even less than the cost of doing it yourself?

If you do it yourself, you will have gained useful skills you can use during your new life as a liveaboard cruiser. Imagine chatting with a fellow sailor who needs the very same job doing in some far-off destination but doesn't know how – before you know it, you've made back half the cost of your own job ... or a couple of beers, depending on the other guy's budget.

If you choose to hire a professional, you may or may not save money on this particular job but it will be done in less time, freeing you up to get on with other tasks. For me, the ideal is to find somebody, a kind of future you, someone who is not a professional but who has the skills and can borrow the right tools. Then do the job with them and learn as you go. The bottom line is, the more skills you have, the better the odds of you becoming a successful liveaboard cruiser. Of course there is always the alternative of investing in a cheap grinder and doing it the low-cost, albeit hard, way. Essentially, every task needs to be considered in this way, and only you can decide on the right course based on your particular set of circumstances in regards to budget, time, current skill set and boat location.

Location, location, location

Our story is one of severe budget restrictions, and so *Faoin Spéir* needed a lot of work. This led to one of our toughest decisions: where would we store the boat while working on it? We rescued *Faoin Spéir* off a trailer, already out of the water and on wheels. The tricky part was that the trailer was not included in the deal (as you'll recall, one of the reasons the previous owner was selling the boat was because he needed the trailer from under her). As we had to transport her from the boatyard, we had a decision to make: do we take her directly to the water in order to work on her afloat or to a boatyard (usually near the water) to work on the hard? Or do we transport her even further inland, to our garden, to work on her at home?

Let's look at what each of the choices involved. Transporting to the water would mean mooring costs, which may not have been too much were we to have moored her on Ireland's inland waterways. So, very affordable, pretty much weatherproof and ideal for working on a project afloat. However, we'd have needed to factor in a 90-minute drive to get to her, plus the cost of fuel and transporting materials to and fro. Imagine having six hours free on a Saturday, only to take half an hour loading the car, an hour and a half driving, half an hour unloading and getting started, and then reverse that to get home again and your six hours results in one hour of work and a fuel bill of £25. Let's assume you travel to the boat twice a week – the fuel bill suddenly takes £2.5k per year out of your budget!

Storing the boat on the hard near the water has the advantage of power and easier access to be able to work both above and below the waterline. However, it comes with alternative challenges and, in some cases, increased costs due to yard fees.

So, having weighed up the options, we chose to transport the boat back to our house and leaned it up against a shed, chocked on the outside. As we described earlier, the initial costs of moving the boat via crane were steep. Had we gone near the water, we could have had the boat lifted into position for a fraction of the cost, since most docks have cranes available by the half hour rather than by the day, which is what we had to settle for.

But once in position, we could use any free hour by simply walking out of the back door and climbing the ladder. If we had to drive 90 minutes every time we wanted to see the boat, there would have been added pressure to make full use of the trip; with the boat in our back garden, it was fine to occasionally climb the ladder and simply sit on the floor for half an hour, imagining how it would all pan out, visualising the end product. Sometimes I would take out an old sailing adventure book and sit in the boat with my back against the bare weave of the GRP and read for an hour.

For three years the boat remained in the garden before we faced the nightmare of moving a large sailboat from the garden of a house on a narrow country road to the sea. Again, the cost was significantly higher than launching the boat from a yard or dock, but overall we had already made savings by having *Faoin Spéir* right outside our back door.

Faoin Spéir sitting against the shed.

Tooling up

Not unlike the debate of DIY versus hiring a professional, the question of what tools to buy and which ones to hire or borrow is going to be dependent on your unique set of circumstances. I was fortunate that Mary had an old mobile home in the garden, which I could convert into a workshop. At its most basic, it meant I could work with larger sheets of timber indoors and out of the elements. It was also useful for storing materials in a reasonably dry store.

Coming from an engineering background, I had a few tools and a good set of basic skills starting out. However, one tool I didn't have, and which my brother donated to the project, was a 30-year-old table saw. When I think of all the tools I used over the course of the project, the table saw probably saw (excuse the pun) the most action. Anyone who has ever spent a long time aboard or working on a sailboat will recognise this issue: the largest piece of wood or appliance on your boat has to be smaller than the hatch will allow. For me, this meant that the widest sheet of plywood panel had to measure less than 90cm. Now, the standard sheet of ply is 4 foot x 8 foot, or 120cm x 240cm if you're working in metric. This meant that every sheet needed to be cut down to a usable size, and the table saw allowed me to do this with relative ease. A good table saw may be expensive, but if you buy a second-hand one, and take care of it, you can sell it on again before you leave for your adventure.

Other than the table saw, which fortunately cost us nothing, the rest of the tools we used were relatively inexpensive. There is a need for a suite of hand tools, and it's worth investing in good ones, as most will be coming with you on your travels. A good set of spanners and a decent socket set, screwdrivers and a couple of hand saws are vital while travelling, so don't scrimp if you can avoid it.

Power tools have dramatically dropped in price in recent years, so it need not break the bank to equip yourself with a mains-powered circular saw and a drill of moderate quality, before you spend a little more on a battery-powered drill and jigsaw. You'll be glad in the long run that you spent a little more on these two tools; they'll make for lighter work and you're likely to carry them on board when you set off.

Unless you're going with a steel boat, then a cheap angle grinder will do, since generally you'll only be using it for a bit of fairing rather than anything heavy duty. Whatever tools you end up with, take care of them, especially when you take to the salt-water environment. A boat can be a very unkind place for tools.

Fitting out

When we found *Faoin Spéir*, she had been completely gutted. You could run your fingers from the transom to the bow without interruption, right along the fibreglass weave. While this meant that there was a lot to be done to turn the boat into a habitable space, it also meant that

After a sweep and a tidy, this was our starting point for the refit.

we could do it in a way that suited our needs. I think the biggest disadvantage of finding a boat like this is the time and materials it takes to get it to a place where we could stay on board. Not even necessarily to live on board, but just to stay on board for a weekend.

The key components were a place to sleep, a place to eat and a place to cook. The easy solution for eating would be out in the cockpit, as there was a table there. However, in the Irish climate and with no cover, we couldn't really depend on this. Cooking required nothing more than a flat surface on which we could use our collection of camping cookers. As for sleeping, this had to be comfortable from the beginning if I was to keep everyone on board with the project. It's not until you start to design and build in odd-shaped furniture that you realise just how much we take for granted. When you go to a chain store to buy a chair for a dining table, it's safe to assume that it'll fit under any table, and be suitable to sit on long enough to consume a leisurely dinner. When you're faced with a stack of wood, screws and an array of tools, where do you even begin to start?

For me, I started with other boats. A visit to the London Boat Show was one of the most productive days we had early on in the project. We set off one frosty January morning, armed with pads, pens, cameras and a measuring tape. Where else would it be acceptable for two strangers to spend the day going from boat to boat, poking, prodding, inspecting and photographing? I was able to measure everything from doorway widths to countertop heights!

Of course, if you're focusing on creating a liveaboard space then, if at all possible, try to reflect domestic living conditions where you can. Many modern boats, even those in the 40- to 50-foot range, are designed for the purpose of a weekend afloat rather than long-term living, so features such as a built-in microwave/convection oven may be a waste of time if you plan to spend most of your time 'on the hook'.

Even mattresses that are perfectly fine for a week or two may become hard and uncomfortable over a prolonged period. We included sprung mattresses on all the bunks on *Faoin Spéir*, mainly because they're more comfortable but also because it worked out cheaper in the long run. Luke and Ella's mattresses are of the sort that you would find in a mobile home; they're 60cm wide and allow for more living space in their cabins. The mattress in our room is the one from the bed in the house because before building the bunks, I took out the measuring tape and designed the base around the mattresses we already owned.

In the Achilles 24, we had a very tight V-berth up forward and needed a mattress for it. We had a spare domestic double-sprung mattress that would do. To make it fit, I opened up the mattress and removed the extra springs, reducing it down to a triangular shape. It may have been a tight space but it was the most comfortable V-berth on the lake.

As mentioned elsewhere in the book, boating costs are inevitably based on what you have at your disposal rather than the retail cost of a professional refit. You can do your own refit for very little, but (and this is at the heart of the *Faoin Spéir* project) doing it on a very low budget will take a great deal of time and patience. But spend enough time looking, and you'll eventually find someone willing to offer you their old oak kitchen for nothing if you're able to take it away – after all, it'll save them hiring a skip. Taps, a sink, drawer fittings – you should consider all these items when refitting. Finding a 'sail-away' project that is complete but needs refitting can be a mixed blessing. Yes, a good clean will probably have you able to spend a weekend on it in some comfort, but replacing rotten sections of the interior or modifying the layout can often be more work than fitting out from scratch. Once again, it's all about compromise. It would be great if you could throw money at the problem, but if you can't, then it's still possible with a little patience, perseverance and imagination.

Unfortunately, there are items you'll simply have to buy, no matter how long you're prepared to wait. For us, I couldn't ever see myself coming across a free stack of plywood sheet, so this was one of those things that just had to be accepted. On the other hand, we needed a cooker, and while the camping cookers were doing their job quite well, the small gas canisters were impractical and expensive. I had considered modifying them to take a regular domestic gas bottle, but the right cooker turned up at the right price. From day one we had been keeping an eye out for a good deal on several items, the cooker being chief among them. After three years, we spotted a £700 model knocked down to £150 on eBay. Two rings, a grill and a reasonable oven – oh, the luxury!

I guess the key thing to remember when it comes to restoring or refitting a boat for long-term cruising is the more time you have, the less it can cost.

Launch day

Ⓜ The day we moved *Faoin Spéir* from our home to Fenit in County Kerry was an exciting nightmare fraught with anxiety. Imagine picking up your house, putting it on the back of a truck, driving it 200 miles and placing it gingerly into the sea!

Faoin Spéir dominated the space in which it stood and was visible for some distance, making it a local landmark. Strangers would introduce themselves to us with, 'Oh, you own the boat!' However, even I underestimated the interest it generated.

It was a beautiful, bright clear day on the morning we moved, and many of our neighbours came to watch the boat being lifted the tiny distance from its resting place to the truck, ready for transport. It was nerve-wracking but the competence of all those involved meant she was soon on the move and heading for County Kerry. Our car broke down en route and we had to abandon it on the side of the road while Leonard's son came to our rescue. Leonard phoned his brother, who saw to it that *Faoin Spéir* was

Lifting *Faoin Spéir* out of the garden.

launched successfully. Although we were not present to witness the event, we arrived to find her floating without her mast. The relief was immense.

Extensive preparation is the key to reducing the stress of moving a boat. Try to move it early in the day, so as to cause as little disruption as possible. If there is going to be traffic disturbance, make sure you give adequate notice to everybody concerned. Ensure that all site planning is done well in advance, in order that the crane and boat transport simply turn up and can make the move efficiently. In this way, you also have a clear plan in your head and moving your boat can be as cost-effective as possible.

Because of the local interest in moving *Faoin Spéir*, and being in the unenviable position of blocking a public road, we informed people of our intentions by placing signs at the gate and including a website address where we had posted details of our plans with an open invitation to visit the boat or contact us with questions. That plan worked very well and generated considerable goodwill and generosity. It's advisable to find a way to communicate your plans to those who may be affected in a similar fashion. Seek any permits you need well in advance.

After *Faoin Spéir*'s arrival at Fenit, Leonard and John saw to it that she was masted, and for the first time in 15 years she was a complete sailboat with a wet bottom. The following day we took her out in Tralee Bay for a short sail. I was terrified and thrilled and relaxed and excited and delighted. How had we managed this? I really had no idea. But here we were, sailing our own boat on the sea – wow! Now in truth she was pretty bare. All the work Leonard had done to that point, which was an inordinate amount, was structural, the foundations if you like. And as anybody who works in construction will tell you, the most important structural work is not visible in the final view of any house, and the same goes for boats. However, never ones to shy away from the deficit in a situation, we planned to sail our boat the 90 nautical miles from Fenit to Bere Island in the south-west corner of Ireland the very next week.

7

Equipping the boat

Ⓛ To make a boat sail from one port to another, no matter how far apart, takes very little. A sound hull, a mast and something to catch the wind is all you really need. There's a saying in sailing circles: if you put the word 'marine' in front of anything, it instantly triples in price. The recreational sailing business is a multibillion-pound industry, and it is in the best interests of the industry that you believe that more is better. The magazines are filled with sailors talking about how they'd never go to sea without some gadget or other. Now, I'm not a purist – I have been accused of being one but really I'm not. I come from an engineering and technology background and I see the benefits of technology every day. Without it, I wouldn't be writing this book and chances are that you used technology to buy or even read your copy. But here's the thing: I love my e-reader, I take it everywhere, and it's ideal for boat life. However, if there's a book I really want to read, and the only way I'll get to read it is on paper, then I'll read it on paper.

If the magazines are full of gadget advice, the sailing fraternity is even more so. I once had a chap visit the boat;

he had pulled up in Bere Island in a Westerly, and a very well-kept boat it was too. I was working on *Faoin Spéir* and we got chatting. I invited him aboard for a look around and the conversation continued. Then he paused and asked, 'What navigation set-up do you have?' I explained that I was going to go with a laptop and GPS dongle, and went on to highlight the advantages of this set-up (low cost, flexibility, plenty of backup laptops, etc). He looked confused, and said, 'All that is very well, but it's not very nautical now, is it?' My first thought was that that may well be the case, but I had a laptop and the GPS dongle only cost me £20. But there is a bigger issue at hand: here is a guy who clearly loves sailing but is caught up in the need to have all the equipment those magazines advertise and other sailors rave about in the yacht club bars.

If we wait until every conceivable condition is satisfied before we cast off the lines, we may well end up waiting too long. Try to identify what is vital to you and your boat. After you have clarified what that is, then you can weigh up how accessible the additional items are or how badly you want them.

As expensive as sailing is deemed to be, the basics are actually well within the means of most. As technology has advanced it has brought with it both the apparent need for more complex equipment with which to sail, and massively reduced the cost involved in the few bits that we *actually* need to sail. A typical example of this is the liferaft.

I can imagine the future gasps from some readers as I write this section, 'Leonard is saying we don't need a liferaft! He's gone mad!' Well, yes and no, I would never suggest that anyone should go sailing without a liferaft. Have I sailed without one? Yes, I have. Have I gone offshore without one? No, I have not. My point is that a liferaft, which has become a standard piece of kit on modern sailboats, makes no difference to whether a boat can sail or not. The boat won't go better to windward if you have a liferaft. So, if we can throw out our liferaft and still go, then what else can we do without?

Wants vs needs

In truth, it takes very little to create a boat that will move with the wind, is watertight and can be steered. All of this could probably be achieved with stuff scattered around the typical house. Where it all becomes much more complicated and expensive is when we start to add the bits that we *want*, rather than *need*. For us it was simple enough: we wanted three cabins, a living area and a head (or toilet). This, I felt, would mean a boat of around 40 feet in length. So, to cross the Atlantic I would only *need* a Mirror dinghy, but I *wanted* a 40-footer. With two children on board, I figured that a centre cockpit would be driest and safest, so I wanted a centre cockpit. Get the picture? This didn't mean that I wouldn't go if we could only find a boat with an aft cockpit within our budget. Rather, we were clear about our desires, and also clear that they are just that, *desires* not absolute needs. A useful exercise is to describe your ideal, and from that ideal examine each detail and ask, 'If this is the only thing I can't have on the boat, am I going to give up and stay at home?'

While we were less inclined to stray too far from a boat of 40 foot, we were able to be much more flexible in other areas. For example, I would love a roller furling head sail, it would make life easier, but in its absence I am happy to continue to hank on and off until the time comes when we get one.

If you decide that you simply cannot go without a 15-inch Garmin chart plotter, then be prepared to spend a lot of money sailing off into the sunset. If, however, you find yourself saying, 'I do want a plotter but what are my options?', you'll find there are plenty of ways to cut the costs. For example, you can spend in excess of a grand on a large-screen plotter, or you can connect a GPS antenna

Our GPS antenna for PC navigation.

to your laptop for as little as £20. Personally, I would not like to go off on a world cruise without a GPS plotter; it just makes life so much easier than guessing your way across the open ocean. So this was one of those things that became a priority, and so I invested the £20 in an antenna for my laptop.

The AIS transponder is another completely unnecessary piece of kit for making the boat go, but one that I needed to make a priority to have on board for my own comfort and peace of mind, even ahead of comforts such as a shower or an outboard engine. I must say, while passing through the Strait of Dover Strait at 2am on a cold November night, the AIS transponder allowed us to focus on the helm and boat rather than having to relay our intentions to the port and shipping over the radio – the moment we made a change of course, they could see clearly our plans.

The domestic side of the boat is no different. We would all love to simply turn on a tap and have all the water we could imagine pour out, but such a supply would become very expensive on a boat. For this you would need a water maker, a pressurised system and the electrics to drive said system, which would involve extra batteries, perhaps a generator and possibly more solar panels. Some cruisers have to run their engine for an hour a day just to run their water maker. The alternative? Bring enough water with you and put a foot pump between the tank and the sink. Yes, you have to be mindful of the amount of water you're consuming but this is best practice anyway, even if you do have a water maker. The savings are huge, as you're not just saving on the initial cost but also on the batteries, engine hours, generators and solar panels, and we haven't even begun to talk about the maintenance on all this extra gear.

In summary, it's great to have all the mod cons but don't let your desires for them become an excuse to stay at home.

M When it comes to needs vs wants, we differ slightly. Leonard would have sailed away in the boat in the condition it was in when we bought it, and the truth is we could have sailed it like that. But I cannot cope with that lack of organisation. I didn't want to sail away in a half-finished boat. I wanted some comfort, and I do not think that is unreasonable. Being able to find things when you need them and being able to stow things safely is a basic requirement to living a normal life as far as I am concerned. So you may find that on a couple's or family's boat, all of the 'vitals' that Leonard speaks of could make for a very long list, but it's a list that must be considered.

Our boat is still a work in progress, and perhaps it always will be. Our first year was spent without a fully functioning bathroom. It drove me crazy. It still drives me round the twist when Leonard starts his 'needs versus wants' malarkey. Of course, I can make do without a fully functioning bathroom on the boat while we are in a marina – I have done for a full winter. But this does mean tramping out in the wet and cold to do one's business, and it is quite miserable. I want a fully functioning bathroom;

I want to get up in the middle of the night to pee without freezing to death ... please?! As I write I am fully aware that this is exactly the point Leonard is making: it's not a need, it's a want, and we are not on a luxury cruise around the world. No. But just because we live on a boat doesn't mean we have to get salt burn every time we want to pee!

The great tender question

The tender, or dinghy, is the small boat that crews use to head to shore after they have moored up or left the main sailboat at anchor. They are usually either hard or inflatable, and can be powered by outboard engine or rowed.

How to go about choosing your tender is one of those age-old questions that really has no answer. I've spoken to many sailors, read many books and imagined many options, and all indications show that the perfect tender does not exist. Unless you can have a tender that resembles Dr Who's TARDIS, which defies space and time, yours is going to make you suffer at times.

We would love a tender large enough to take all four of us, a week's worth of shopping and a couple of guests from the pier to *Faoin Spéir* anchored 2 miles away in the next bay over, and once we arrive, to be able to throw it up on to the deck without either breaking our backs or covering the windlass. But our dream tender, alas, is just that: a dream.

One of the key questions that you need to ask yourself when considering a tender is how do you intend to moor. If you tend to tie up in marinas at the end of the day, then you may not even need a tender. If you anchor, or spend your time on swinging moorings, you'll probably use your tender every day. If you do intend to use a tender on a daily basis, then it's worth making sure it suits your needs. A family such as ours requires a tender with a larger carrying capacity than that used by a solo sailor. There are few who advise against getting as large a tender as you can comfortably stow on your boat. However, there are many who would argue about its construction.

Hard or soft?

When acquiring a tender, there are two main categories to choose from: an inflatable dinghy or a rigid one. There are good things to be said of both, but it really comes down to personal taste and circumstances. If you want a small boat that you can power under sail, engine and oar, then only a rigid tender will do. If you are limited by stowage, a rolled-up inflatable will be easier to stow.

Which tender should you go for?

Inflatable

Pros

- light and easy to launch or drag up a beach
- stows into small space relative to carrying capacity
- tends to feel less 'tippy' if you're transferring nervous guests

---

- naturally fended for times when the big boat needs to be nudged or pushed into position

Cons

- tricky to row in weather
- needs an engine for regular use in varied weather
- can take a lot of effort to inflate and so it may not be available in a hurry
- does not like to land on rocky shores
- is a favourite of thieves due to its engine/tender/lightweight combination

Rigid

Pros

- GRP tenders are usually quite tough
- generally handles better in the water
- available and ready to go at a moment's notice
- may take a sail

Cons

- stowage takes a lot of space
- can be heavy and awkward to launch
- that 'tippy' feeling may unnerve your guests
- needs fending when coming alongside the big boat

For us, as with most of the decisions we had to make, our choice of tender came down to cost versus features. An outboard engine will run to several hundred pounds, whereas oars are a much cheaper and more reliable alternative. With this in mind, an inflatable was out, as

Luke, endlessly bailing the dinghy.

they don't handle very well when being rowed. The other feature I was hoping for in a tender is that it be sailable. And so, based on the cost, the space on our deck and usability, I opted for a Mirror dinghy. Now, the Mirror is in fact 10-and-a-half foot long, and we actually only have 10 foot between our mast and windlass. But it seemed too good an option to forgo without trying.

Emergency equipment

Sailors regularly discuss what safety equipment they have on board, which they would not go to sea without and which they feel could be left behind. In all of these discussions, the only piece of gear that everyone agrees should be on board for every passage is the lifejacket. I have never encountered a sailor who does not value its place on board. When the conversation moves to sailing offshore, every long-distance cruiser we have ever spoken to considers the liferaft and flares essential.

Lifejackets

Lifejackets are an essential safety feature of boat life and any chandlery will be happy to help you select the best ones for your crew and your budget. Spend as much as you can on lifejackets; they will literally save your life. Here are the main things you should consider when using lifejackets:

- Lifejackets should fit properly and be fastened correctly at all times.
- Make sure children have lifejackets suitable for their weight and height.
- Crotch straps should be fastened appropriately.
- Store lifejackets safely.
- Service lifejackets annually and when they begin to deteriorate, replace them.
- Carry extras on board for visitors or in case of loss, theft or damage.

It is important that each crew determines the rules to be followed regarding the wearing of lifejackets when on board, when using the dinghy or at the marina.

On *Faoin Spéir* we have our own rules. Once underway, if you enter the cockpit you must wear a lifejacket. Anyone leaving the cockpit to go forwards must wear a harness and be tethered to the jackstay.

The laws themselves vary from country to country on when and where lifejackets should be worn, often based on the size of the boat or the particulars of where you are sailing, but one thing you can be sure of, no jurisdiction has ever insisted that you don't wear your lifejacket!

The liferaft

The laws and regulations for liferafts on leisure vessels also vary wildly depending on which country you explore and, at any one time, they usually seem to be up for review in one form or another. In the UK, a liferaft is not required so long as the vessel is used in a strictly non-commercial manner. However, the easiest way to satisfy all potential requirements is to equip your boat with a raft and maintain an up-to-date service certificate. It need not cost the world; we do our own servicing and send the CO_2 bottle away for testing to a specialist company. The cost during our last service (2016) was £40. Laws aside, if you are sailing offshore (beyond safe range of land in your tender), and in particular if your boat is a family boat, then we really do recommend you keep a liferaft on board.

There are two important points to consider when equipping your boat with a liferaft: can it accommodate everyone on board and is it stowed in an accessible location? There is little point in having your liferaft buried at the bottom of a locker beneath one of the forepeak berths, and it would make for a very awkward conversation if there wasn't room for everyone to climb aboard in an emergency!

The brand is less of an issue, as the manufacturing and provision of such equipment is extremely heavily regulated, so that the quality of all the well-known brands is of a very high standard. We carry an Avon four-person liferaft on *Faoin Spéir* – it came with the boat and was manufactured in 1984. The disturbing thing was, it hadn't been serviced since 1990. I certainly was not prepared to take a family to sea with a liferaft that had gone without a service for 24 years. So, we decided to see if it was worth even having serviced by pulling the cord. The valise itself did not inspire confidence, looking like a punch bag that had gone one too many rounds, but the cord was in perfect condition. One swift tug later, I was treated to a reassuring pop and hiss as the bag transformed into a perfect little orange tent in the garden. It was as though it had been packed only yesterday. Once the raft had fully inflated, which took only 10 seconds, I checked the whole thing over for any signs of escaping air, rubber degradation or corrosion of the inflation hose fittings. No evidence of any problems. Even the knife for cutting the cord was perfectly sharp (you can see a video of this inflation at our website, www. FaoinSpeir.com).

The liferaft functioned perfectly almost 30 years
after its manufacture.

The raft was in excellent order, inside and out, and
there in the middle of the floor sat a green canvas bag,
filled with survival goodies. For the most part, the fully
stocked kit was in good condition, with the exception of
the perishables. The cans of water, all dated 27 June 1983,
were well past their best, the flashlight and its accompanying
batteries had combined into a very unpleasant lump at the
bottom of a plastic bag and the flares had gone out of date
in 1991.

However, all non-perishables (included a fishing kit, a
signalling mirror and a repair kit) were perfectly serviceable
and even in 'as new' condition. We left the liferaft out for

three days where we inflated it, with very little reduction in air pressure, and certainly nothing that we could not rectify with the manual pump supplied in the kit. The performance of the liferaft after all those years is a testament to the build quality and standards of safety equipment at sea, and as a result I worry less over the possibility of a non-deploying liferaft that has been regularly serviced. However, I would still not trust my life to an out-of-date liferaft anywhere outside of the safe confines of the garden.

Flares

Flares fall into the category of items that you hope you will never have to use but when you do need them, you *really* need them. We carry a set of flares typical of most long-term cruisers that we know. Stored in a waterproof container, we have four Red Parachute Rockets, four red hand-held distress flares and two buoyant smoke-type flares. Each type has its own specific uses.

Red Parachute Rocket

This flare is primarily an attention grabber. It is launched to an altitude of about 300m and can be seen for up to 30 miles. While it will give potential rescuers a direction in which to head, it won't allow them to pinpoint your position with any accuracy. Although the burn time is typically less than a minute, the 30,000 candela against the backdrop of the sky is hard to miss.

Red hand-held flare

Once you have gained the attention of a rescuer, and they can be seen approaching, you should use this short-range distress signal to highlight your exact position. As the name indicates, this flare is ignited and held aloft in your hand. Unlike the parachute flare, the distance at which the flare is visible can vary greatly depending on the position of the person holding it aloft and the sea state. Standing on the deck of a boat will give a far greater range than if you are in the unfortunate situation of operating the same flare from a liferaft.

Buoyant smoke flare

Unlike the previous two flares, these do not produce a light signal and so they are ineffective at night. The bright orange smoke signal produced is highly visible from the air, contrasting effectively against the water. It serves well as a position marker and wind direction indicator for helicopter rescue personnel.

LED flares

Hand-held LED flares have been around for several years now, and although the early versions were not really fit for purpose, the newer models have proven to be visible up to 5 miles away at night. Concerns have been highlighted in the press as to whether the red LED light of the flare can be distinguished from a portside nav light over such a distance. There are no such worries about a pyrotechnic flare, such is the ferocity of its flame, although the LED version does have the advantage of longevity; not only do they have an unlimited shelf-life but when pressed into action, they operate for hours rather than a minute or less. The current cost (in 2018) of this advantage is around £100, so for the moment Mary and I will stick to the traditional pyrotechnic flares.

While each of these flares is intuitive to use, it is worth taking the opportunity to ensure that everyone on board understands which is which and how each one functions. Most training centres run survival at sea courses that include the use of flares. The Royal National Lifeboat Institution (RNLI) in the UK and Ireland often runs workshops on flare handling, as does the US Coast Guard. See the Useful Resources section for relevant contact information.

Electricity

The electrical system on board *Faoin Spéir* is not unlike that of most small boats. We have a way of generating power (solar panels, engine) to charge batteries. The batteries then go on to supply a 12-volt DC circuit (for lights and navigation instruments) and a 240-volt AC circuit (via an invertor) for what we call our 'house sockets'. For us, the sockets are of the three-pin square variety used in the UK and Ireland as standard. We went with this type because our appliances were all of British/Irish origin.

It may well be a matter of life and death that the electrical system on your boat is correct and within the

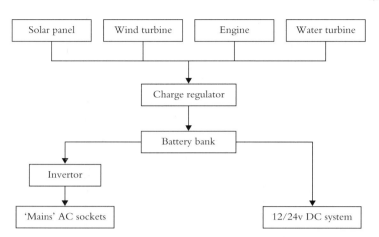

Electrical system onboard.

specified guidelines. To ensure this, I would recommend that you invest in a dedicated book on the subject, for example Mike Westin's *Replacing Your Boat's Electrical System* (2013). For our purposes, we will stick with a simple system diagram.

On *Faoin Spéir*, our preferred initial source of electricity is via our solar panels. They are quiet, clean and, beyond the initial purchase price, completely free. We have two solid 120-watt panels attached to the pushpit and one flexi 80-watt panel, which we connect when moored. This totals 320 watts that are fed into three 110-amp batteries via a 30-amp regulator. This set-up has proven sufficient to serve our needs as a family of four with four laptops, four mobile phones and a TV, although I must admit, the TV is only run for about four hours a week. Either way, we have ample electricity to keep us going through a British winter.

Faoin Spéir's solar power set-up: three panels, totalling 320 watts.

Cost of providing electricity on *Faoin Spéir*

Solar panels: 120W solid panels, £90 each. 80W flexi panel, £70. Total = £250

Batteries: 110 amps, £90 each. Total = £270

Regulator: Solar 30, £20

Invertor: 500W, £80

Extras: Wire, connectors, etc, £30

Total cost: £650

The less electrical equipment that we carry on board, the less electricity we have to generate and store. If we discount the likes of electric kettles, hobs and ovens, which really have no place on a sailboat, one of the biggest consumers of electricity on a boat is the fridge. Mary and I have spent many evenings weighing up the fridge question and I would say that 90 per cent of long-term cruisers suggest not to bother. One couple we know set out with a fridge and once it broke, they never fixed it. Now it's just another cupboard.

For me, a number of factors came in to play. Chief among them was of course the cost. If we built a fridge, we wouldn't lose too much space. It would sit nicely against the hull, and we could even have a little freezer box. But the cost was simply too much to bear. It's not necessarily the price of the refrigeration unit itself – although at £400 for a basic model I thought of how far that would go at anchor – the problem is that it doesn't stop at the initial £400. Once installed, I now need to generate more energy to run said fridge, via an additional three solar panels at least. What about when the sun goes down? Yes, batteries. I don't want to tax one too much, so another two 110-amp leisure batteries would be required. Add to this the extra wiring, regulators and fittings, and my £400 solution is not seeing much change out of £1,500. All this before I start looking at maintenance on the system and the time and effort that goes into installation.

Suffice it to say, we don't have a fridge on board *Faoin Spéir*. This does not (surprisingly) mean that we can't enjoy a cold beer; I've left a small locker under the waterline free from insulation. We treat this space as we would a fridge, and it has worked wonderfully thus far. In practical terms, it keeps food for as long as it takes us to consume it; sliced meats, cheese, butter and UHT long-life milk (once opened) have kept for three days in this space. Past this we would be inclined to discard anything open that long, but in truth, it would be a rare occurrence that such perishables would go more than two days without being used up completely with four hearty appetites on board. Now, I have to admit that the further south we travel, the less cold the beer tends to be. But I figure that if in the future we absolutely need a fridge, then we will revisit the problem. For now, we are getting on just fine.

Showering

I don't think I've ever met a sailor who didn't appreciate a good shower. However, for most, a good shower only ever happens ashore. The most common shower arrangement on modern sailboats is tank-fed via a water heater, the shower hose and into the holding tank or drained out through the hull, all driven by an electric pump. This arrangement works very well and is often a match for domestic showers. The downside is the amount of water consumed. I was just reading about a popular 44-foot boat currently on the market. The freshwater capacity is 330 litres and the electric water pump is rated at 19 litres per minute. That's less than 20 minutes of showering in the tank. Put a family of four on board and you'll soon have to start seeking alternative showering solutions.

We looked at many options when fitting out *Faoin Spéir* and while I love Hal Roth's solution of a plant sprayer, pressurised by the attached pump handle, we settled on something that on the outside resembles a domestic shower. We use a recycling system that involves a 'sit in'-style bathtub from a mobile home, a bilge pump and a shower hose. This allows anyone (especially teenagers) on board to shower for as long as he or she likes in 5 litres of water. I'm sure many of you are thinking what has often been said to us: "That's gross. You're showering in your used shower water!" In reply to this, I always ask what happens when you take a bath.

So the routine goes something like boil a kettle, mix with cool water to the right temperature, pour into the bathtub and switch on the pump. Eventually the water

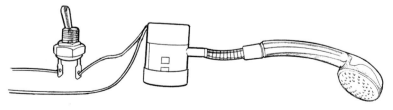

Basic circuit of *Faoin Spéir*'s recycling shower.

does go cold, but at that stage it's time to get out anyway. To empty the tub, I had considered a rather convoluted valve system for pumping overboard, but instead we simply turn off the pump, move the shower head to over the toilet bowl and switch on the pump again to empty the water via the toilet. There is a little water left behind when all is said and done but nothing that a small towel doesn't soak up in one go.

Of course, when the sun is out there's nothing like a solar shower on the deck, although getting the soap into all of those ageing crevices might prove a little embarrassing.

The smartphone

The lightning-speed developments in technology over the past 20 years have been spectacular, and many of these developments have filtered down to the liveaboard cruiser. We were once described as 'hardcore' and 'purists' because of our decision to keep the boat systems simple. But my route into sailing has not been a traditional one; I didn't grow up in dinghies, no one in my family sailed and I didn't set foot in a sailboat until my mid-30s. I learned to sail through the writings of Knox-Johnston, Moitessier and Slocum. They talked of navigating the world's oceans, battling storms and keeping a boat moving safely. The technology at their disposal was the same as was available to Nelson. And this should be the starting place for any sailor inclined towards serious cruising: to develop the ability to sail your boat from A to B without electricity, because if you sail far enough and for long enough, someday it will happen.

So, with this as my starting point, I'm a firm believer that you should evaluate each piece of technology on its merits. As you can tell from other sections of this book, I'm a huge fan of our AIS transponder system. Time and again it has delivered peace of mind. But beyond this, I do find myself increasingly turning to my smartphone.

These little computers in our pockets have transformed cruising. So long as you have the electricity to charge them, the benefits are many. We live in an era of ubiquitous mobile data connectivity, where often the signal several miles off the coast is even better than that in town centres. Granted, offshore the signal is lost, but even then your smartphone will give you a set of GPS co-ordinates in an emergency.

The array of applications available to the cruising sailor is mind-blowing, and on a typical day I reach for mine for weather updates, anchor alarm and contact details for the local harbour master's office. Chatting with one marina owner about approaching boats, she said that their staff don't really man the VHF radio any more because if they can't be raised on the radio, the boats always phone on their approach. I'm not sure I agree with this development but it is how things are, and to stubbornly stick solely to VHF may well compromise safety.

Let's take a closer look at some of the more popular smartphone apps for sailors.

Weather apps

This is an obvious one, and there are many excellent weather applications out there. While I like to use *Windy*, it really is a matter of personal preference. If at all avoidable, I would never use my phone to access weather information for passage planning. It's simply too small for me; I prefer to bring up the animated weather models on the laptop screen from several sources and then arrive at my own interpretation. But for an easy-access weather overview and update, the phone is excellent and we use the weather app daily.

Anchoring apps

The anchor alarm function has been around for some time on electronic plotters and in computer-based navigation software, and a wonderful aid to both safety and sleep they are too. Upon dropping the anchor, you click the anchor alarm function and the desired radius of chain. If the boat moves outside that circle, the alarm sounds to alert you to a possible dragging anchor.

With the advent of the smartphone application, we have a low-power alarm that sits next to the bed and keeps an eye on our position while we rest. There are many apps to choose from but, generally, the simpler the application, the less power it consumes. Make sure you test its accuracy, which is easily done by rambling about on land or, as I have done more often than I care to admit, rowing to shore with the alarm screaming from some inaccessible pocket or other, indicating that I'm more than 30 metres from the anchor!

Navigation apps

Like the weather, I dislike the idea of using a smartphone for navigation but have found it useful for quick overviews. We use *Open CPN* on a laptop with a GPS antenna as our primary electronic navigation system. *Open CPN* also comes as a free application for the smartphone. I've not loaded the maps on to the phone, but even without them it will give me a readout of my speed over ground (SOG) and course over ground to the next waypoint (COG). In fact, it made a really very useful substitute when I was sailing and the log sensor became fouled, thus leaving me with no speed registering in the cockpit (a useful thing for adjusting the sails). Of course, having to go below to check the speed is no great chore but how handy it was to stay put. I recall another occasion when we were sailing upriver in the very busy port of Cork. Our destination was right in the centre of the city when, two hours from tying up, the laptop died. Our AIS was still functional and putting out our position, so I accessed the marine traffic website and there we were. Again, it's not the end of the world to navigate a well-marked river with paper and eyesight, but our little purple triangle online added an extra layer of security to our passage.

Transport and travel apps

Along with the obvious advantage of being able to find and book public transport on a smartphone, a subtle, yet useful development is being able to generate digital boarding passes for air travel. Although we do carry a printer on board, not everybody does, and even then it can be a nuisance retrieving it from storage and setting it up. Now we can check flights, book them and have our boarding passes on our smartphones in an instant if we need to make a trip by air. No more digging out the printer, or racing about looking for an internet cafe or library in which to print tickets. More and more bus and train services are adopting the same principle, and those that don't usually facilitate the collection of tickets at the station.

Entertainment

M Aside from safety, navigational and electrical equipment, one of the most important considerations for you long-term cruiser is entertainment. We spent many hours prior to departure converting our library of DVDs and CDs into digital formats and now we have a vast store of movies and box sets on external hard drives. There are many software applications available for this very task, most of which are free. I'll not mention any specifically here, as they seem to come and go as quickly as technology advances, but I'm sure if you consult your nearest teenager, they will advise you on your needs.

You can pick up an external hard drive of about 1 terra-byte (1Tb) in most computer or electronic stores for less than £100 and this will store about 700 feature-length movies. Based on our viewing of two movies per week, that is enough to keep us going for almost seven years! It can be a very valuable currency among cruisers to swap films and box sets from your library, but a word of caution: there is a considerable amount of pirated material making the rounds and some countries take such offences very seriously.

We also have a 32-inch, flat screen smart TV on our boat. Gone are the days of the power-hungry tube televisions that took up as much space as the galley cooker, for modern TVs can be wall mounted, protruding less than 2 inches into the cabin. Power consumption is also a fraction of that required to run its older brethren, with our particular model drawing less than half a watt. The smart features allow us to connect the external hard drives directly to the television for viewing movies and listening to music. It also allows for the connection of a laptop so that we can display our passage navigation. This is usually of great interest to non-sailor guests who may be visiting.

To complete the technological entertainment suite, we carry a Nintendo Wii games console. To be honest, it doesn't see much use, but having one on board was a useful selling point for Luke and Ella. If you are considering a games console for your boat, the likely choice would be one of the 'big three': PlayStation, Xbox or Nintendo Wii. Leonard made the choice based on power consumption, with the Wii using a paltry 85 milliamps, less than a quarter of the needs of other two.

Although we own a TV, we do not have access to TV channels. We get our daily news online and occasionally we watch documentaries online too, but the vast majority of the time we prefer to read, play Scrabble or chat.

e-books

One of the greatest advances in technology for the liveaboard sailor is the e-book. We all have e-readers on board, and aside from the fact that we can carry thousands of books with us without taking up any space, there are many books available for free in electronic format. A lot of authors produce free samples of their books so that you can read a chapter or two before committing to buying them, and many more give away the first book in a series for free in the hope of enticing you to buy the others.

For me, aside from the space that it saves, one of the biggest benefits to owning an e-reader is that there are thousands of books that are no longer under copyright and are available for free from several online sources. Probably the most notable of these is Project Gutenberg, a service in which volunteers began converting public-domain books into electronic formats long before e-readers ever appeared on the market. Fancy a bit of Tom Sawyer? Or maybe a little Plato? Or how about a recipe from a classic cookery book? They have them all, and with the e-reader, all you need is a brief connection to the internet and some free time to read.

Board games

Aside from reading, one of the most popular spare-time activities on board is a good old-fashioned board game. I know from speaking with other boat folk that we're not alone in this – every boat seems to have its own favourite. For us, it's usually Scrabble, and I recognise that many of you will think it sad that this may be a highlight on board, but just try it. Find a board game that you can enjoy (chess, Ludo, Monopoly, Connect 4 and Trivial Pursuit are all classics for a reason and battery-free) and play once or twice a week with friends or your significant other. Add a glass of wine or a beer, a bowl of crisps and some friendly competition, and you've got yourselves a great evening's entertainment. It may take you a while to find the right game but that is part of the fun.

We carry a variety of board games on the boat. One thing we have found is that the boxes for many games are unnecessarily large and so we have removed most from their boxes and now store the playing pieces in zip-lock bags and the boards on our bookshelf.

The ship's log

Maintaining the boat's logbook may be a royal pain to some. The idea of filling in the book every time you pop out for a three-hour sail around the bay can seem tedious. I have to admit, that while sailing on the lake in the Achilles, I didn't keep a log. I had no instruments, so the rows dealing with wind and boat speed would have been nothing more than a best guess, and as I was sailing much the same route each time I went out, the pages would have looked like carbon copies, save for the dates. Once we launched *Faoin Spéir* and began sailing in salt water, however, we kept a log every time we went out. There are four very sound reasons for keeping your logbook up to date.

1. For pleasure

In the immediate aftermath, a great day's sailing is fresh in your mind and it can feel as though you will remember every moment, who was there or how the fishing was, forever. But months of years after the event, it can be hard to recall whether a particular passage occurred in June or July. A well-kept log, therefore, will allow you to revisit a memorable passage and enjoy it all over again. We chat elsewhere in the book about 'firsts', and the logbook is where you can find them. When it comes to personal pleasure, or recording memories, the logbook is not just for next week or next month – I hope to be thumbing through our old logbooks into my 80s. When we fill our logbook, we keep this in mind. We don't stop at wind, speed and bearing; we add short notes like 'We sighted a huge shoal of tuna feeding on squid'. These are the snippets that will trigger the memories for years to come.

2. For the boat

The logbook is a very useful tool for recording maintenance issues that crop up while underway, such as a squeak from the windvane or a noticeable stiffness in a winch. Many problems only show themselves while the boat is actually sailing or motoring, and they may be such that they are not so urgent as to need immediate action, but may well be forgotten once the boat is at rest at the end of the day.

The logbook is also where you should record the running total of miles covered, hours underway and engine hours. If your oil filter needs changing every 200 hours of motoring, your logbook will tell you when. Moreover, should the day come when you wish to sell your boat, the prospective buyer would be delighted to see that you kept such logs.

3. For training

It is advisable that any sailor who wishes to progress through the ranks of sailing certification should keep a personal logbook. This would include all passages complete with durations, destinations, hours at sea and duties carried out on board. Most training courses or sailing exams require previous experience (so many miles in tidal waters, X number of night passages), and the way this is verified is via a personal log signed off by the relevant skipper. For most liveaboard cruisers, and for families in particular, the boat's log serves this purpose. If in the future either Luke or Ella wish to take a Coastal Skipper exam, our logbook will serve as evidence to satisfy the prerequisites.

4. For the law

Before you panic, I don't know of any country where the skipper of a cruising leisure sailboat is required by law to keep a logbook. Having said that, it is not unusual to be asked to produce one if the coastguard or another maritime official comes aboard. It makes life easier for everyone if an official can flick through the log to see your recent ports and who has been on board. Either at home or abroad, a well-maintained logbook shows that you sail in an organised and seamanlike fashion. Chances are that this will be enough to satisfy the authorities, and they will bid you a safe and pleasant voyage. If, however, you shrug your shoulders when asked for the logbook, you might well be in for a prolonged visit.

Much more serious than having to entertain the coastguard with tea and biscuits is proving your competence in the aftermath of a collision or other calamity at sea. Investigators, be they from an insurance company or the Department of Agriculture, Food and the Marine, will want to establish that the skipper has taken all reasonable precautions and exercised his duty of care for the boat, her crew and her passengers. The first place to look? The logbook. Not only will a well-maintained logbook demonstrate due diligence around the occurrence being investigated, it will also show a track record of adherence to seamanlike practice.

8

Equipping the crew

M All too often, the focus of the prospective liveaboard is on the boat, the destinations and the costs therein. But we must also ask ourselves, 'How ready are the crew?' Can they each tie a bowline? You may be surprised on closer inspection by the holes that appear in one's own knowledge and that of the rest of the crew. Whether you're just starting out or have several Atlantic crossings under your belt, there's always room for improvement.

Training and study

L The topic of training and certification is not unlike that of equipping the boat. I mentioned in Chapter 7 that whether or not a boat has a liferaft, it is not going to affect whether or not said boat sails. The same is true of crew qualifications. Whether I have a commercial ocean Yachtmaster certificate or a pat on the back from the old guy down the pier who has never untied from the pontoon, what I know about sailing has not changed. Granted, the more qualified you are, the easier it is to charter etc, but if you haven't completed a course, it doesn't automatically mean that you haven't completed the study and training.

When I left the relative safety of the lake and moved out to the ocean, I had spent the previous four years sailing our Achilles 24, usually solo and always without an engine. I learned a huge amount – sometimes the easy way and sometimes the hard – about the behaviour of a boat in relation to winds and currents. By the time we sold her, I could thread her through marinas and stop her on a penny. I didn't have any certificates to say I could do this, but it's hard to imagine any novice having just completed his/her five-day Day Skipper course being more skilled than the chap in the folk boat who's made thousands of passages around Britain's coast.

One of the great freedoms that still exists in the British Isles is that of sailing a boat for leisure without certification. However, if you wish to sail beyond those waters, it is more usual that you will need a 'driver's licence' of sorts. The Royal Yachting Association (RYA) Day Skipper certificate will generally suffice.

Although most developed countries have their own governing body responsible for sailing certification, the majority base their standards on those set by the RYA. The RYA has more than 2,400 licensed training centres across 58 countries, and having issued more than 250,000 certificates in 2017 alone, it is the accepted international standard for sail training and certification worldwide. The table below shows the RYA's recommended progression route for your typical cruising sailor.

Progression route for a typical cruising sailor (courtesy of www.rya.org.uk)

Course	Assumed knowledge	Course content	Ability after the course	Min. duration	Min. age
					Recommended
Start Yachting	None	Introduction to sailing and seamanship	Basic knowledge of yachting	2 days	8
Competent Crew	None	Basic seamanship and helmsmanship, navigation and meteorology	Able to steer, handle sails, keep a lookout, row a dinghy and assist in all the day-to-day routines	5 days	12
Day Skipper	5 days, 100 miles, 4 night hours Navigation to Day Skipper Shorebased standard and basic sailing ability	Basic pilotage, boat handling, watch organisation	Able to skipper a small yacht in familiar waters by day	5 days	16
Coastal Skipper	15 days, 2 days as skipper, 300 miles, 8 night hours Navigation to Coastal Skipper shorebased standard Sailing to Day Skipper standard	Skippering techniques for coastal and offshore passages	Able to skipper a yacht on coastal passages by day and night	5 days	17

CRUISING

In general, the minimum requirements for chartering a bare boat are either the International Certificate of Competency (ICC) in Europe or the International Proficiency Certificate (IPC) in the USA. You can obtain either by completing the five-day Day Skipper course and submitting the related certificate to the relevant body in your country of residence. What many people don't know is that instead of completing the five-day Day Skipper, you can apply to sit the ICC exam and skip straight to the ICC licence. If you have the skills, this is a faster and cheaper route to the same end. Never once have we been asked for any qualifications beyond the ICC.

It's hard to argue with the mantra that you can't beat good instruction from a qualified authority, and it is something that I subscribe to. I would suggest, however, that the most 'qualified authority' may not always be on a commercial course and even if they are the most qualified, are they delivering the instruction that you actually need in a way that suits you?

Too often I have heard of people attending courses, and not just sailing courses, being rushed through the tick boxes and out the other side with a stamp on a form that suddenly says they are ready to be let loose on the world. This can sometimes be even more dangerous than not receiving any training at all.

While there is no question that securing instruction from a qualified authority is the best way to learn, just remember that there are many ways to access such an authority. Learn and study as much as you can, equip yourself with enough knowledge to ask the right questions, and when you have been given the answers, question those while seeking new approaches to reach your goal. The key to the entire project for us, the reason that we could afford it, is rooted in this philosophy.

Everything that you need to know is out there and mostly available to you through books and magazines, and while you must adopt careful judgement while reading or watching anything online, videos and podcasts – especially those produced by professional sailors, sailing associations and liveaboards – are a great place to start. Even a stroll down a pontoon and a chat about the boats with a random sailor will lead to all sorts of insight. Leave your ego behind, accept that you know very little and ask the stupid questions – I've never been met with anything but helpful advice from other boatowners. If you can avoid getting caught up in the bravado of daring feats of sailing heroics, then you can learn an awful lot from a weekend of pottering around on a small boat in safe water with the right people.

Key skills

There is nothing quite like getting stuck into a bit of sailing, out on a boat with the wind and waves, to improve your skills. Many of the most important of these can be learned and honed without you ever leaving the comfort of your armchair. I'm not suggesting that there is any substitute for practical application, but navigation, passage planning and knot tying do not require a boat. One of the things I love about these vital skills is that from the very moment you decide you want to live on a sailboat and sail off around the world, you can immediately start working on the tools that will take you closer to your goal.

Knots

I'm trying to imagine a sailboat without knots and I simply cannot conceive of it. Despite the development of all manner of shackles, clasps, adhesive tapes and bindings, nothing has come close to replacing the knot on a boat. Some knots, like the masthead and the monkey fist, have become more or less obsolete and ornamental through the advances in modern equipment but, regardless of her size, from a coracle to an oil tanker, a sound knowledge and practice of knots is vital to safe operation. Simply put, if you wish to sail, you need to know your knots.

Whether you use a piece of clothes line, a tow rope or even an old shoelace, there are a handful of knots that you can start working on immediately to help you become a better sailor. I would start with the king of sailing knots, the bowline, before moving on to the clove hitch and the reef knot. From here you can expand your knowledge by learning to tie them in different situations, such as on to a ring, over a post or through a cleat. Beyond these key knots, I would commonly use a figure-of-eight stopper or loop, a sheet bend, a Prusik and a sheepshank.

These days you don't even require a book of knots (although I do love a good knot book). Everything you need to know is online, or you can download free knot apps to your smartphone. Whatever your approach, random pieces of rope scattered about the house or in your desk drawer at work will have your knot-tying skills improving daily. You can get started by learn how to tie the bowline, clove hitch and reef knot right now (see pages 289–296).

Navigation

Like knots, navigation is not an optional extra to the sailing lifestyle but, unlike knots, there are some costs involved before you can make a start. If you have ever successfully used a road map in an unfamiliar area, or better still, taken part in orienteering, then you are well on your way to using a nautical chart. The commonalities between land- and water-based navigation are many. Both are north-up orientated, two-dimensional, overhead views of the region through which you wish to navigate. Both use scale and internationally agreed symbology to make distance and features. While both contain information on heights both above and below sea level, maps will focus on the 'above sea level' information while charts tend towards the 'below' bits.

The main difference comes into play when we move from exploring the virtual world of the chart and map into the real world. On land, our route from A to B is generally well marked along paths and roads. At sea, these routes range from 'less obvious' to 'non-existent'. Add to this the complicating, often significant factors of tide, current, leeway, compass deviation and seabed topography, and your head will soon be spinning. The pressure of accurately extrapolating a safe route for your family from all of these parameters (before we even mention the weather) might seem too much. In time, you will learn all that you need to know, just don't try to learn it all at once.

Paper charts

I am yet to meet a sailor who doesn't like to view their potential route on a paper chart. I have to admit that underway, I use the electronic chart more often, but there is nothing quite so reassuring as planning your route on paper. Aside from actual tide times, paper charts contain all you need, including restricted areas, tidal overfalls, flow rates of currents, depth, obstacles, lights and buoyage.

There are several publishers to choose from, and few would argue that the Admiralty charts are the most popular. However, at the risk of offending some sailors, I do not like the Admiralty charts. They are very fine and well proven. They have found a home on most of the merchant and military ships around the world, such is their excellence. Yet, for the yachtsman I have found Imray charts to be more suitable. They fold flat into A4 plastic sleeves and stow rather more easily on a small boat than the insufferable rolls from other providers. You can also get Imray charts on water-resistant paper, and they each contain notes particularly relevant to the small-boat cruiser rather than for general shipping.

Charts that fold to A4 size stow much more easily.

Some of the finer points of paper-based navigation can be tricky, and the easiest way to gain the necessary knowledge is through attending a classroom-based course. I've not attended one, but I do know from my days as a teacher that being in a class and learning with others is a great way to iron out any fuzzy bits when dealing with theory work.

If classwork is not for you, there are many training centres offering distance and online courses in navigation, among other topics. Though it means that you won't have an instructor in front of you to answer specific questions, you can usually access a tutor via email or telephone. Most online courses suggest that you equip yourself with a copy of the *RYA Navigation Handbook*, by Tim Bartlett (2014). At a cost of under £25, it really does contain all that you need to know for cruising and is definitely worth having in your library.

Electronic charts

Try to avoid falling into the trap of learning your navigation on a plotter. Once you see how easy it can be, it'll be hard to motivate yourself to really understand how it transfers to paper charts. Remember, the day may come when all you have is the paper chart, and that won't be the best day to learn how to use it. That said, electronic navigation is a wonderful addition to any boat. The technology has become so sophisticated that it will do all of the calculations for you and spit out a heading, or even communicate directly with the autopilot. This unnerves me a little but maybe I'm just old-fashioned.

More and more sailors are turning to their iPads and other smart devices for navigation. However, if you sail enough, you can almost guarantee that your smart tablet will break or fall overboard at some stage. These devices are not designed for the sea, so please ensure you have a backup (paper or otherwise).

We, and many other long-term cruisers we have encountered, use laptop computers for navigation. One of my favourite downloads is *Open CPN*, which is a free electronic navigation package developed by programmers who sail and sailors who program. It can run on your PC, tablet or phone. We use *Open CPN* as our primary backup to paper charts. It runs on the laptop with a GPS antenna connected via a USB.

One of the great advantages to using a package such as *Open CPN* is that you can take Google Earth images and overlay them. So, for parts of the world where chart data may be lacking, you can combine the chart with satellite or aerial images to get the best available information. Using this method, I often find myself doing some armchair navigating in far-off parts of the world that we hope to visit in the future. You can find out more about *Open CPN* and the relevant downloads at www.opencpn.org.

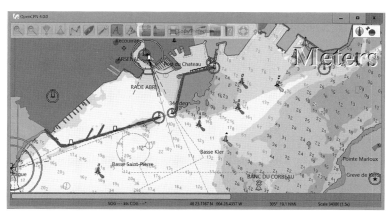

Screenshot from *OpenCPN* navigation software running on our laptop (image courtesy of opencpn.org).

Passage planning

Now you're ready to combine all you know to create a plan that will get the boat and all on board safely from A to B. Passage planning is a skill that improves with practice but it doesn't require a boat to develop. Many people will already have useful transferable skills in this vein. Anyone who has planned a camping trip, festival weekend or even a long drive to visit friends, for example, would have engaged in some form of travel planning (although, in some ways it is easier for a liveaboard cruiser than a festival-goer – you don't have to pack and you can't have left your wallet at home!).

Assuming that your navigation is up to the task, the two other key factors are the weather and provisioning. Both of these are covered in more detail in Chapters 10 and 16, but here I want to outline how you can develop these skills without ever leaving your armchair.

Navigation is best done as a couple, a crew or even with a few like-minded friends. Decide on a virtual trip between two ports – they don't need to be too far apart, as sometimes the shorter trips are the toughest to plan. Now decide on a departure date and agree on some specifications for the virtual boat. Everyone can take a day or two to put in a little research and come back with a plan. Here are some important points to consider during the planning stages:

- high and low tides (times and heights) at departure and destination ports
- sunrise and set, moonrise and set

- boat draught and typical speed
- weather (wind direction and speed, visibility, air temperature)
- ocean swell height and period
- intended departure time and expected arrival time
- need for watch rotation and skill level of individual crew members
- provisioning, fuel, water
- required documentation and available services at destination

You would be amazed at just how much of the above can be answered instantly via an internet search. Once everyone has completed their plan, check it against the actual weather on the proposed day. Pick a point and time on the virtual passage and ask yourself if each person on the crew would be able to deal with the live conditions. After completing this exercise a few times, you'll soon find yourself developing intuition around forecasted conditions, and whether or not they'll suit your boat and crew.

Non-boat skills

In a book that covers all aspects of living on a sailboat, it may seem a little strange to say that many of the skills needed to make a success of it are not directly related to sailing. Those skills, such as cooking, provisioning and budgeting, all belong in the realm of good housekeeping,

143

but on a boat they are vital to the heath, happiness and general well-being of everyone on board. DIY know-how is also crucial to any long-distance cruiser; if you plan to do anything beyond port hopping, the ability to conduct repairs on the go will make life easier and safer, not to mention more cost-effective.

If you are currently dreaming of boat life then, along with surrounding yourself with charts, ropes and sailing books, go to a local market, buy some fresh produce and learn how to cook it without referring to a recipe book or website. If all goes according to plan, you may one day find yourself in a land of unfamiliar fruits and vegetables with neither internet access nor a Delia Smith to hand, and nothing but your wit and your galley to save you from a hungry few days until you can find someone willing to sell you a cooked meal. OK, so it may not come to that but cooking, even when pottering around the coast close to home, is vital to a successful transition to living aboard.

Aside from the aforementioned skills, communication skills are also a key component of running a successful cruising sailboat. They are usually your first defence if you run into any difficulties. Suppose you do find yourself in that market of unfamiliar fruits and vegetables – chatting with the locals will generally help you sort out the plantains from the bananas.

Of course language is useful, but it's even more useful to have a pleasant and cheerful demeanour. I can honestly say that since moving on to the boat and sailing off to a life less usual, I have found that a smile can reduce your living costs by hundreds of pounds in a year.

Ⓜ In the category of non-sailing skills, being able to live in close proximity and work as a group is hugely important. It is so easy in the present day to think the individual reigns supreme but, in truth, on a sailboat everybody contributes to safety, good humour and keeping things ticking along nicely. Problem solving, good communication and a little self-awareness and crisis management also contribute to a happy boat. You might not have particular expertise in the area of sailing, but if you are good in a crisis or can keep calm in a situation where a problem has to be solved, you could be a very valuable crew member.

Apart from being able to produce tasty, nutritious food underway, which is a super skill that is much appreciated by all except those suffering with seasickness, being able to sew also comes in very handy for mending sails and crew attire. Finally, being able to catch and gut fish makes you very popular on most boats, especially on *Faoin Spéir*. Thankfully, I live with three fisher-folk, so all I have to do is cook the catch.

First aid as a long-term cruiser

A knowledge of first aid is a necessity for boat living. There are always bumps and scrapes and insect bites to be tended to and managed. Every parent knows that if your child has a rash you immediately do the tumbler test to check if it is meningitis, a heat rash or an allergic reaction, and you act accordingly. How do you know this stuff? It's your duty to know it; you learn as you go and life teaches you. And if you're unsure, you can consult your doctor and all will be well. However, living on a boat means that you do not always have access to a doctor, so you need to be able to make the call yourself.

It is advisable to have a complete health check with your doctor prior to departure and make him/her aware of your plans to travel. If you have any health issues, you should always follow your doctor's advice and agree on the methods that will enable you to fill out prescriptions and participate in ongoing screening while you sail.

First aid training

I recommend that all adult members of the crew have a certificate in first aid. There are many avenues to access first aid training; your local library should have a register of the organisations you'll need to access it. Many of these organisations will train you in return for you giving them some time as a volunteer. Workplaces are another avenue for first aid training and certification but be aware that they can be workplace specific. Certain companies also supply first aid training for a fee, the advantage of which is that you can usually select from a 'training menu' to suit your needs. Maritime first aid courses deal specifically with medical emergencies at sea; check with your local yacht club, which may run one annually.

If you have never tended to first aid needs, you may want to start simply and build up your skills over time. I suggest selecting a course that includes defibrillator training, as this is a very specific skill in resuscitation and many newer yachts carry a defibrillator on board. You may wish to consider running through the basics of first aid with your children, too. After all, knowledge is power.

First aid kit
The next thing you need to consider is your first aid kit. The contents will be determined somewhat by your intended passage. I wouldn't consider it necessary to carry antibiotics on board in continental Europe, as you're never too far from help, but if we were heading across the Atlantic for 21 days I would consider them essential. I know a lot of long-term cruisers who travel with a supply of antibiotics, and this makes sense if you're sailing in areas of the world where medicine is in short supply or difficult to access. If this is the case for you, then it is absolutely essential you know the circumstances in which to use this medicine and the medical history of the person you are treating. David Werner's *Where There Is No Doctor* (1973) is not only a great read but it also has a wealth of information on the subject, and is a useful book to have on board.

There are many excellent first aid kits available on the market. There are also several suppliers of marine first aid boxes, which are pretty standard but when you add the word 'marine', you automatically triple the cost! Therefore, my advice is to buy a standard first aid kit and adapt it to your needs.

Additional items to add to your boat's standard first aid kit

Antiseptic cream or gel

Burn gel or aloe vera

Extra bandages, including support bandages for minor sprains

Waterproof sticky plasters

Skin glue

Suture kit

Sterile water

Non-alcohol wipes

Analgesics, ibuprofen or paracetamol, including those suitable for under 12s

Cough medicine (non-drowsy)

Throat lozenges

Arnica cream and tablets

Antihistamine medicine

Calamine lotion

Antifungal creams and powders

Extra disposable gloves

Thermometer

Cold packs

Large safety pins

Splints, both large and small

Electrolyte solution or powder for children
Syringes and hypodermic needles
Emergency dental repair kit
Antiseptic mouthwash
Vaginal yeast infection cream
Cystitis tablets
Antibiotic cream/s
Seasickness medications and motion sickness bands
A clean pair of scissors

I have included seasickness medication in the list above, but actually we don't carry it on board at all. Luke has occasionally suffered with seasickness, but regardless of how rough the conditions, sitting or lying down with the lee cloth in place while taking regular sips of water has proved to be the best medicine, while others say focusing on the horizon helps.

Whatever you choose to include in your kit, keep it in an accessible place and ensure that all crew members know where that is. It's also useful to keep a log of the medicines consumed on board – we have a large first aid kit and we maintain and review it regularly. We also have a smaller one to hand during passages, which contains a little of everything. You must decide how to manage it on board your boat.

First aid emergencies
In truth, the vast majority of first aid emergencies on board are pretty similar to those on land, and include cuts, burns,

bites and bruises. Sticky plasters, aloe vera, arnica cream and tablets, paracetamol, antiseptic wipes and cream/s, calamine lotion and an electrolyte solution will probably cover most of what you encounter. In the tropics, extra caution is advised as high heat and humidity can lead to the rapid spread of infection.

When you arrive in a new location, I recommend speaking to the locals about potentially poisonous or biting species, such as insects and snakes, especially if you're travelling in an area that has different breeds to those with which you grew up. If there are snakes, find out where locals go to get treated with anti-venom should they get bitten. Use a language app if there are translation issues. While you're at it, ask them which fish are safe to catch and consume and which are not.

In the case of mosquitoes, prevention is better than cure. Ensure your boat is well protected by hanging nets over beds, hatches and ports. There are excellent battery-operated insect repellents available, too. Burning citronella oil or candles in the cockpit helps to reduce the numbers of winged visitors in the evening.

It is well documented that any cuts, wounds and stings acquired in the tropics should be cleaned and covered as soon as possible, as infection spreads very quickly. You should also deal with all cuts or stings acquired while swimming or paddling in tropical seas or other waters immediately. Irrigate the cut, suture it if necessary and keep it covered. Then keep it dry while it heals. It is good practice to check children every evening for any cuts or stings because they may not always report them, or even notice them.

Medical help

If you need medical help, seek it. It does become trickier as a cruiser, so when you arrive at a port we advise you to go online and search for medical services in the area. Alternatively, conduct your research on medical facilities as part of your passage planning.

If you have a medical emergency in an area that does not have a resident doctor, that poses a bigger problem. Here are several suggestions for dealing with emergencies at sea:

- Check with locals where they get their medical support (again, remember to use a translation app if there is a language barrier).
- During opening hours, a local pharmacist is a good resource.
- At anchor or mooring, put out a radio call for assistance or ask the question of other cruisers.
- Phone home. Phone a doctor, hospital or clinic in order to relay the symptoms and request assistance.
- Use a search engine to find the closest source of help.

9

A place to stop

M A funny thing happens when you tell people you live on a sailboat: they imagine you constantly being at sea. Of course we are not constantly at sea. If we total the number of days we sail each year it would average out to about 50, meaning that we spend more than 300 days at anchor or berthed in a marina or harbour. We tend to not sail through the winter, preferring to 'settle' for a few months and get to know the locals.

Berthing

The term berthing is used to describe attaching your boat to land, whether that is tying to a dock in a marina or to a harbour wall. Being able to simply step off the boat has several advantages; proximity to services such as showers and laundrettes are my two favourites, but of course supermarkets and public transport are also much more accessible. There is also the presence of other sailors and the possibility of getting to know people and making new friends. When we left Ireland, initially I was very lonely due to leaving behind my good friends, neighbours and family, and I do miss them. But now I have confidence that wherever we go we will make connections with new people. Why do I feel so confident? We have done it over and over again at this stage, in many new countries and in new languages, too.

Berthing also allows you to be connected to land with the freedom to move on whenever you wish to do so. The only disadvantage to berthing is the potential cost, which can sometimes be prohibitive; we have heard of marina costs from £10 (Spain) to £100 (Italy) per night for a 12-metre boat! However, there are usually special rates for winter berths. Public harbour or town quay berthing tends to be very inexpensive and, in some cases, free. We wintered at the quay in Port Launay, a little village in Brittany, France, for the princely sum of £1 per metre per month – that's six month's winter berth on the River Aulne for just £72. Therefore, my advice is to do your research (one idea is to check out the marina on Google Maps) and call ahead.

Long-term berthing at a tidal quay

Ⓛ It was in Port Launay that we learned a valuable technique for keeping the boat safe against a tidal quay. Having travelled 17 miles inland up the River Aulne, and through the first lock on the Nantes–Brest canal – a beautiful stone-lined waterway – we found that many of the boats were stood off from the quay wall with long stakes fore-and-aft.

153

At first I thought that the wall was eating through fenders of long-term berths, but a local explained what it was and why we should do the same if we were staying a while. This section of the canal was tidal. During high spring tide, the water would rise above the quay wall and boats that were not stood off or attended to would at best scrape along the wall as the tide fell (leaving their fenders sitting, impotent, on the quay) and at worst find themselves high and dry on the quay.

There were two lessons to be had here: the first was learning how to rig standoffs fore-and-aft for a flooding quay, and the second was remembering to examine local boats, and to follow what their owners do.

Using the standoffs to good effect on a high spring tide
in Port Launay, France.

Part of the challenge of this arrangement is in finding attachment points for your stakes at the quayside. You may be lucky and find rings or bollards in precisely the right position, but chances are you'll need a little more flexibility. This can be achieved by running a chain (in our case, an anchor chain) from one ring/bollard to another alongside the boat. The weight of the chain has the advantage of keeping the quayside end of the stakes below the level of the quay, thus offering more support.

We used 75mm square posts that were 3 metres long, trimmed a little to a length that suited our particular situation. At the quayside end, we attached each post to the chain via a nut and bolt. At the boat end, I used some webbing that we lashed and screwed in place. The

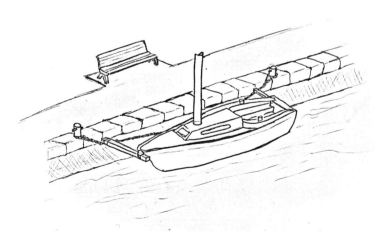

Symmetry will help to keep the boat parallel to the quayside as it rises and falls.

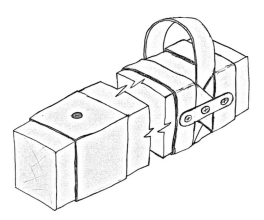

The arrangement at each end of our stand-off stakes.

webbing loop allowed the flexibility needed to tie off to the boat.

With this arrangement, *Faoin Spéir* could rise and fall with the tide without taxing her fenders or scratching her sides. Of course, in the interests of full disclosure, we learned these lessons the hard way.

Mooring

M We had done quite a bit of sailing before we started mooring, and tying up to a mooring buoy is a very different experience altogether. Usually there is a mooring field with many spaces to moor, a bit like a painted car park, where the buoys denote a space and if it is free, you may park there. Although the visitors' mooring buoys come in different shapes and colours around the world (for example, yellow cylinders in Ireland, white cones in France), they are all basically an anchored buoy bobbing up and down to which you tie your boat off to keep it in one position. The boat moves around into the wind and it is very comfortable, if a little disconcerting at first.

Mooring may be free in some places but in others you may need to pay a small fee to the local authority. If a person in a rib looking for money does not approach you, there are usually instructions at the quayside on how to pay for your space. I like mooring; it feels more secure than anchoring and more private than berthing.

Anchoring

Anchoring, on the other hand, frays my nerves. It has all the uncertainty of mooring, except there is no end point. When we set anchor, I am usually at the helm, following instructions relayed back through two people, since I cannot hear over the noise of the engine, and invariably I reverse the boat or give her throttle at the wrong time. I can just never seem to get it right.

After we eventually get the anchor set and the correct amount of chain out, that is when the real nerve-tingling begins. We use an anchor alarm and this genius piece of modern technology allows us to hear, by way of a loud, repetitive noise, if the boat moves outside of the alarm perimeter. Leonard can then quickly assess whether, for example, the boat is dragging the anchor and is therefore unsecure, or if the tide has dropped and we have too much slack. All I know is that during the first night at anchor, Leonard doesn't sleep a wink and actually sets his alarm clock if the change in tide occurs during the middle of the night. This is extreme dedication to our safety and the safety of others, in my opinion.

While we have had some tense times at anchor, there have also been several really excellent experiences, like the week we spent in Stangate Creek in the Medway River in the Thames Estuary – what a lovely peaceful spot!

Ⓛ It seems that every generation has a preferred anchor and every crew swears by its own choice. Let's be honest here: if you don't have faith in the anchor you're carrying, you might as well just give it away, for you won't be sleeping a wink.

Over the years, I've heard sound arguments for each of the common anchor types, from spade to plough and from fisherman to modern hybrids that defy description. There is no question that most modern designs are superior to the old guard. Today's computer modelling and testing equipment has allowed for the evolution of design features that were simply not possible in the past. I would argue, though, that an no amount of clever design can make up for poor anchoring technique. Before considering upgrading your anchor, make sure your anchoring technique and knowledge is first fully upgraded. Study and practice are the cheapest ways to improve your boat's holding at anchor.

Anchoring pop quiz

You have just completed a 14-hour sail and go to anchor in a bay with a long, sloping seabed of sand/mud. It's two hours to low tide and the greatest range for the next few days is 3 metres. You draw 2 metres, so for safety's sake you decide to anchor in 4 metres with plenty of sea room. How much chain do you put out?

Let's see, maximum expected depth will be about 6 metres and with a scope of 4:1, you're probably thinking of putting out 24 metres of chain.

Theoretically you'd be right, but if you have plenty of sea room, and you're looking for a good night's sleep, don't scrimp on the chain. The bottom line is, if the 3:1 or 4:1 rule makes for good anchoring, imagine how secure you will feel if you can put out 6:1 or 8:1?

In general, we try to anchor away from other boats, giving *Faoin Spéir* plenty of room to swing. We let out about a 4:1 scope initially, and allow the anchor to dig in and the boat to settle. We set the anchor alarm and leave the electronic plotter on while we have a cup of tea, or something a little stronger, depending on the previous sail. After about an hour, the plotter tells us the fully story of the boat's behaviour and from there we can make decisions to adjust or reset the anchor. If I'm happy with everything, I'll go forwards and let out more chain before bed, typically up to 6:1, before adjusting the alarm and getting a good night's sleep.

With this method, we have only ever dragged when we have expected to drag, and sometimes dragging is the best option. A good example of this was when we were leaving the Thames Estuary after a wonderful winter on the Medway. It was 11pm and light was becoming scarce. We planned to position ourselves at Ramsgate for a Channel crossing to France but had little wind that day. Rather than engaging the iron sail, we cruised slowly at about 2 knots in the sunshine for 12 hours and opted to anchor off Margate for the night. There was a great deal of big shipping in the anchorage, which made me a little nervous, so we headed west along the coast for half an hour where we found nothing but large pebbles on the bottom. While our Bruce anchor (see more on types of anchors below) was without equal in the Medway (known locally as the 'Mudway'), it is simply not designed to cope with such large pebbles. After four attempts to dig in and with the last whisper of light on the horizon, we moved about a mile offshore and managed to bite. There was no way that we were going to hold – whatever we had a hold of, it was only going to last until the change of tide.

Examining the tide times, I set my alarm for 1.30am and within five minutes of climbing out of bed, we were dragging as expected. Rather than rousing the crew,

The bulk of the work to Faoin Spéir *was carried out in the heart of farming country, miles from the sea.*

She looked a sorry sight when first nestled against the shed at the foot of the Galtee Mountains in Ireland.

Sometimes nothing but graft will get the job done.

This was the first 'passage' as Faoin Spéir, *50 metres to the pontoon.*

David and Leonard out on the mirror dinghy in Lawrence Cove, Bere Island.

Jim Rueff and Linda Davis, who lived and voyaged on Faoin Spéir *for 15 years, travelled from the USA for a reunion with their former home.*

The crew of Faoin Spéir *with close friends and fellow liveaboards.*

We met the wonderful Sea Cadet training ship TS Royalist *in the Isle of Wight, and Luke and Ella were treated to a tour.*

Voyaging on a boat is not all about the sailing.

Right: Communal dinners and barbecues are a great way to socialise and learn the local language.

Blue skies, seas and a clear horizon.

Left: Mines, of course, are best avoided, unless they're like this one – which the RNLI have converted into a collection box.

Mary, helming out of the Thames estuary.

The Pegasus Bridge on the short canal leading to the heart of Caen, Normandy, France.

Emergency at sea, when we lost the helm 15 miles off the south coast on our first attempted crossing to the Isles of Scilly.

Some of the finest dining in the world happens on the foredeck of Faoin Spéir.

and weighing anchor, I checked our position to ensure we still had a mile clear all around from land, shallows and shipping. I then set the anchor alarm to a 150-metre radius and allowed the Bruce and 50 metres of chain to drag and catch, drag and catch throughout the night until sun up. I tracked the night on the plotter and in total we had dragged 60 metres in five hours. It was not my best night's sleep, but in those circumstances it was better than probing about in the dark for a soft spot that may never have materialised.

Which anchor?

There isn't a great deal we cay say here that hasn't already appeared in a multitude of other sailing sources. Every sailor (and many non-sailors) have opined about which anchor is best, and I would say that they are all right! They make their arguments based on how comfortable they feel using their preferred anchor and their knowledge of its weaknesses. So – and it's worth repeating – first and foremost perfect your technique. After this, I would say size matters. You can make up for a lot of flaws in anchor design with size and strength. There are a few signs that tell us when a nearby boat is a liveaboard cruiser, and one of them is that it is sporting a comically large anchor. You can get by on anchor watch for a couple of weeks at a time, but when you're a liveaboard on the move, you need security while you sleep. So, assuming your technique is sound and you are equipped with a sizable lump at the end of your sizable anchor cable, let's have a look at some of the more popular anchor designs.

The Bruce

Why am I starting with this one? They don't even make them any more and yet they are still very popular. With good reason. In the interest of full disclosure, the Bruce is my personal favourite. We started using our 15kg Bruce because it was the anchor that came with *Faoin Spéir*, and I figured if it was good enough for her previous liveaboards during their 15-year occupancy, sailing in two oceans and in three continents, it would be good enough for us. I do have to admit that I would like a larger anchor, but for the moment our cruising kitty doesn't permit this luxury.

The Bruce anchor.

The Bruce was originally developed for holding oil platforms, and as such works very well when exercised from a constant direction with a constant strain. It stows nicely on the bow roller, but I wouldn't want to be carrying on deck or finding locker space for one. There are copies out there but an original is an investment; I have seen people pay twice the price of a new copy than for an original Bruce.

CQR
A clever play on the phonetics of 'secure', the CQR is one of a long-standing breed of plough-style anchors. While chatting about anchors one day, a good friend once asked what ploughs do. And that sums up the CQR for me: it does tend to dig and turn over the seabed in a rather slithering motion. Originally designed for holding seaplanes, the

Our CQR anchor.

CQR has always received high praise from the likes of top sailors such as Tom Cunliffe and Bill Cooper, and with an endorsement like that, who am I to argue? We carry a 22kg CQR on our bow, nestled alongside the Bruce and ready for dispatch at a moment's notice if we need a backup. I'm conscious that it's a lot of weight right where I don't want a lot of weight, but we're not racers. We cruise at a walking pace and love a good night's sleep. As with the Bruce, the CQR has good pedigree and it is worth looking for the genuine article.

The Danforth and the Fortress

These anchors are lightweight-type anchors, or LWTs. The Danforth is the original, and was designed in 1940 by Richard S Danforth. The Fortress takes lightweight to the next level, as it is constructed from aluminium magnesium alloy.

It's hard to pass over the positive attributes of a Danforth design. It stows flat, has good holding in a constant direction for its light weight, is easily handled and deployed and it doesn't cost the earth. I wouldn't want to have one as my sole anchor for long-term cruising, but as a kedge for your typical liveaboard, there is a lot to be said for having an LWT close to hand, mounted on the pushpit and a handy warp ready to go.

Scoop and spade anchors

Scoop and space anchors are part of the new generation of anchors. They include the Rocna, which was developed by New Zealander Peter Smith in the mid 1990s. I've heard great things about them. One cruising couple mentioned how they started to see people arriving in popular anchoring grounds, whereupon they would toss out an anchor like a bag of rocks before cracking open a beer. On further investigation, it was Rocnas as far as the eye could see. I don't care-how good an anchor is – it could be a core-boring robot anchor for all I know – you must always apply good technique, every time.

Long-term anchoring

As a long-term liveaboard cruiser you will, I hope, find yourself in places that you wish to stay in for longer than a week. Spending a few months or even a year in one spot provides opportunities that are lost to those passing through. Language ability, friendships and community involvement deepen the longer you stay.

If you are laying at anchor for long periods in one place, it's worth putting in a little extra effort. A good starting point is to speak to the locals. They can tell you about the seasonal variations and what to expect in exceptional weather and tide combinations. Remember, if you are anchoring for several months, you are not just anchoring for the current conditions but for the worst possible conditions that particular area may see all year. If a stationary mooring is out of the question, two anchors will see you rest easy.

The possible configurations are varied, depending on the available sea room, the tidal flow and the geography of the surrounds and seabed but, essentially, one of the following three layouts will most likely suit your needs.

Tidal estuary

This applies to anywhere that the current changes with tidal regularity. If you are laying at a single anchor and the tide changes direction, the anchor will usually lift, turn and dig in again. They do this with remarkable consistency and falter very rarely, but falter they do. If you remain in the same spot for long enough, there is a good chance the boat will, at the very least, start to nudge its way increasingly further from your initial starting point. We won't even mention the worst-case scenario. One good solution to this is to set up two anchors, one upstream and one downstream, for each direction of flow, and joined by a length of chain that measures at least twice the desired scope. You can then shackle the chain

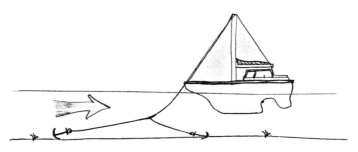

Long-term anchoring in a tidal river or estuary.

166

that goes to the boat (the overall length of which should be at least that of your desired scope) to the centre of the anchor chain.

A small point to remember when anchoring in a tidal zone for long periods is that rudder position can impact how the boat shifts from one place to another. Generally speaking, if you have the helm over to one side or the other, the boat tends to circle about the chain. Depending on your shackle arrangement, this can cause the chain to twist, which shortens the scope, ultimately pulling up the anchor. While this is not an issue over the short term, it pays to be aware of how your boat is behaving on the turn of the tides so that you can find the ideal rudder position for long-term, harmonious anchoring.

Non-tidal river

Here, a single anchor that is well dug in to good holding can stay put for years, but for longer stays, particularly if you are leaving the boat for extended periods, a second anchor will give you great peace of mind.

I've seen two techniques used to good effect in this scenario: two anchors parallel, forming a triangle with the boat as the third point; and, less commonly, both anchors and the boat all in a straight line. You may decide on either based on space, chain availability or simple preference.

To lay two anchors in parallel, we first lay anchor one as normal, letting out our 4:1 scope. Once we are satisfied that that anchor is well set, we motor up to and a little forward of the position for our second anchor. We then allow the flow to bring us back as we pay out chain. Don't pay out the full length just yet; what we want to do is set the second anchor independent of the first. Once the second anchor is set and holding, we can pay out the remainder of our predetermined chain for anchor number two. If all looks well, we can adjust each chain so that the boat is sitting on an imaginary line, perpendicular and crossing the centre point between the two anchors.

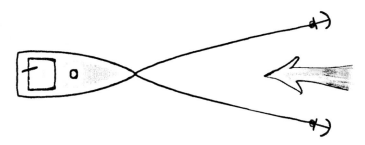

A second anchor in parallel is ideal for when you need extra assurance.

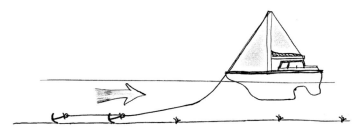

In a stiff blow, or long-term anchoring in a bay, it's hard to beat the simplicity of two anchors in series.

Dropping two anchors in series or in line follows much the same process as dropping a single anchor. The important thing is to ensure that you give enough space on the chain so that the anchors don't foul each other – 5 metres would be good but 10 metres better and, ideally, you would measure your scope from the second anchor (the one closest to the boat). The major advantage to this technique is that the second anchor on the chain keeps the drag on the first on the horizontal.

Tight spaces

This is probably my least-favourite deployment of two anchors. It's not that it's inferior or questionable in any way, I just try to avoid it and by avoiding it, I am less practised. There's a lesson for me there, I think. Anchoring fore-and-aft. It's ideal in tight spaces, preventing the boat from swinging.

The execution is straightforward, in that you drop and set one anchor, usually your bow. Then you would leave out enough scope to bring you over the stop where

Fore and aft anchoring for tight spaces.

you wish to drop your second anchor, taking in the cable at the bow while leaving out at the rear until you have achieved your preferred balance and position. Try to avoid this technique where you might have a tidal flow on the beam; I've yet to see an anchor react happily to being pulled sideways.

10

Provisioning

Provisioning is an essential component of life at sea, especially if you are at anchor or making longer passages. As a long-term cruiser, it is likely that you will not have access to a car, so you'll need a stock to fall back on for those times when access to a shop or market is out of the question.

Before we became cruisers I had read quite a bit about provisioning the boat and feeding the crew, along with watching a video by that doyenne of American sailing, Lin Pardey. I even attended a seminar on the subject (I was very conscientious!). To that end, we provisioned the boat in accordance with what we had read and heard. That initial provisioning served us well; it allowed us to travel between four and six weeks with minimum restocking. But among the successes we did make some mistakes, both of which we'll examine in this chapter.

We were eager to learn from the experiences of those long-term cruisers who had gone before us – if they had successfully lived the life we were aspiring to, then surely they were to be emulated. Nowadays, there are people out there who look to us in the same way. However,

I caution against it, my friends. As we have mentioned elsewhere in the book, sailing and its associated skills have remained more or less the same for thousands of years, but technology has completely changed almost all other aspects of cruising life. We can now order almost anything online and have it delivered to a parcel hotel for an agreed fee, practically anywhere in the world. That is the advantage of consumerism.

The impact of the internet

How does this apparent detour impact on provisioning your boat? Traditionally, ships were provisioned in great detail and with volumes of salted this and dried that in order to prevent scurvy, rickets and all kinds of dreadful seafaring diseases. Today, our tastes can be much more varied. With the flick of a button we can order a can of Heinz baked beans to our nearest virtual postal address. Alternatively, we can go online to find the location of and directions to the nearest supermarket within an hour of arriving in port. The internet has proven to be a wonderful thing when stocking up.

However, I do caution against relying on technology for all your provisioning needs. On our first visit to Camaret-sur-Mer in France we spent two weeks in a marina and for the first week bought our bread and meat in a small shop on the quay, paying a little over the odds and bemoaning the lack of a decent chain supermarket to better suit our budget needs. But when we checked online, we just could not find a supermarket! We puzzled about this, as Camaret-sur-Mer is a jumping-off point for crossing the Bay of Biscay, so we felt sure it would have a decent spot for topping up on provisions. We were there four or five days and were headed to the post office to send our letters home, when, lo and behold, we turned the corner and there was the giant store of a well-known supermarket chain. It was not listed on the very popular search engine, but there it was, nonetheless. Always remember, technology may make life easier in many instances, but it also pays to spend time exploring on foot.

Crew tastes and needs

Everything I had read about provisioning said to stock the boat well, stuff every available space with food, avoid bringing packaging on board, and watch out for weevils, cockroaches and other minibeasts. Of course, I was going to bow to the superior knowledge of experienced sailors. But I failed the one test of preparation that all these sailors highlighted, and that is to know your crew and prepare for them.

Food

You know your people, you know their tastes and the volumes of food they can consume. Food assumes an extraordinary importance at sea – it is not just nourishment, but heat, taste, companionship and, in some cases, salvation. Food becomes power, it revives the drooping spirit but it also fuels it with superhuman ability in the face of fatigue and exhaustion. It is imbued with hope. On a wet, drizzly morning after 20 hours' tossing about at sea a bacon sandwich with fresh white bread and a hot mug of tea or coffee is rocket fuel. Therefore, provisioning becomes a fine art.

It might seem obvious, but having a few tricks up your sleeve, like a surprise treat, can turn a wholly miserable situation into a bearable one. When we are underway I calculate the number of meals I will need to prepare at sea, taking into account both crew and trip duration, and the ingredients and utensils I'll need to prepare said meals. I stow these separately so that they are readily available for me to prepare food in all sea conditions. But rarely do we need to prepare food in a storm; Leonard's motto is 'I like to sail without spilling my tea', and as much as possible we adhere to that. As a result, cooking is easy enough. This is one of the benefits of living aboard and cruising – we can choose when we leave port and tend to do so only when conditions are favourable.

Once you have decided upon meals and snacks for your crew, you will need to move on to water, drinks and alcoholic beverages.

Water and other drinks

Water is an essential. We all know this and we carry water, like all sailboats, in our water tanks. Checking water levels and keeping the tanks filled may seem obvious but it is a learning curve. On land, for the most part, you just turn on a tap and there the water is. Living on a boat, water becomes an obsession; we're always thinking about how much we have for washing dishes, flushing the toilet, showering and domestic use. Calculate how much water you use at home every day and divide that by 100, and that is how much we have on board, never mind how much we use. Therefore, we are extremely frugal with our water.

In terms of other drinks, we carry concentrated cordials and milk. UHT long-life milk makes for excellent storage without refrigeration and powdered milk works extremely well in both cooking and baking (not to mention in our super coffee (see page 225)!).

Alcohol

Neither Leonard nor I drink very much, but we always have a small stock of wine, beer and Irish whiskey on board. Alcohol is an international language and there is nothing nicer than sitting out in the cockpit in the sunshine and enjoying a drink with new friends.

Medicine

Medicine is another essential on board a sailboat and we have a well-stocked first aid box (see Chapter 8).

Thankfully, we have not had to use it much but it is crucial to be prepared at all times. I just hope I am never in need of first aid, as Leonard is a bit squeamish, so I would be relying on the children for assistance.

The practical side of provisioning

All cruisers are different

As with most aspects of the cruising life, your budget will dictate how you provision your boat. I know many sailors reading this book will be familiar with the aforementioned Lin and Larry Pardey, an American couple who've circumnavigated the world on a low budget and who advocate sailing for all. They, like many sailors, follow their own dream in their own way, and they advise that individuals follow *their* dreams according to their own means and desires. I have heard anecdotally that the Pardeys set out on one of their circumnavigations with no money whatsoever but with enough food on board for four months. I love the freedom of this philosophy. Lin Pardey puts it best when she says, 'Get out, plan a dream and go for it.' Would I be able to live like this? Absolutely not, my anxiety would be through the roof. So while I aspire to the freedom to be able to live like this and the implicit assertion that all we need is food and water, I encourage you to provision your boat as much as your budget allows.

Restricted space

So how should you go about provisioning for cruising? First, you must consider your boat's size and storage capacity. At this point, also consider your facilities. What type of cooker or cooking facilities do you have at your disposal? Do you have a fridge or cold compartment? This is crucial, as it influences the kind of provisions you purchase. For example, if you do not have an oven you can reduce your stock of flour, as the likelihood that you'll be baking bread and cake is drastically reduced.

This raises another important issue: the capability of the cook. If the cook is a baker, you are going to add a significant amount of flour to your provision list. If not then you might replace the flour with the more expensive instant bread mix, which takes up more space and is considerably more expensive. Of course, you could also do without bread altogether on longer cruises or while at anchor.

Convenience and long-life foods

In my previous life, I was of the opinion that convenience food held little merit. However, as with so many other aspects since I became a cruiser, I have had to revise my thinking. When provisioning your boat, I suggest you buy a variety of tinned goods that you can open and heat with ease in even the roughest of seas. Be sure to test them out one at a time before you buy in bulk. Why? So that you're not left with 20 cans of tinned sludge not fit even for a cat (we speak from experience).

You may want to consider supplementing your food store with stock cupboard and dry essentials from the following list:

- long-life and powered milk
- eggs
- nuts of various types
- dried pulses, such as beans, lentils and chickpeas
- sugar
- spices, stock cubes and herbs of all types, and as much as you can carry
- oatmeal
- fats, including oils and butter (preferably in tubs with a lid)
- tinned fish of all descriptions
- tinned tomatoes, vegetables and fruits, as well as the fresh variety
- dried pasta, rice and semolina
- syrups, jams, marmalade and honey
- tea and coffee
- crisps

If you have a freezer and a fridge on board then you can also carry meat. We don't, so we only buy fresh meat and cheese when in port. For longevity and taste, we use cured sausage, such as chorizo and salami, which is delicious on pizza, and used in pasta and omelettes.

Occasionally we also carry chocolate, but we try not to have too many treats on board as we are weak-willed!

Finding your own balance

Ⓛ I love food, it's as simple as that, and so when the thought of heading off in a boat for good first popped into my head, the thought of how I was going to feed myself immediately followed. Our ideas about provisioning, formed initially through reading and chatting with saltier souls than I, turned out to be wise words indeed but not entirely right for us. Speaking for our specific situation, and it's not an unusual one, stocking the boat to the gunwales with tinned and dried produce was not the way to go. It simply wouldn't make sense to fill the boat with food for a month for a family of four before leaving Ireland … only to sail to England, where food in the supermarkets is cheaper.

I can understand why older cruisers advised us to stock up with everything from chocolate to antibiotics, from bits of string to spare pencils, but the reality of cruising in today's globalised world is that there are few places left where provisions cannot be found. As one meanders about the coastline of any of the continents (save for Antarctica), you are never far from a butcher, baker or general grocer, and if you are willing to eat as the locals do, you'll probably save money to boot.

Once we got a feeling for our life aboard, we found an approach that fits very well with our cruising style.

We sail with a general route in mind, moving from port to port until we find a place that clicks with us. Here, we may stay for two weeks or six months (we've given up trying to predict – we simply know when it's time to move on). Before moving on, we ensure that the boat is stocked with canned and dried foods, hardy vegetables, eggs and cheese – enough to feed us for a week or two. We take on a couple of days' worth of perishable fresh produce (remember, we don't have a refrigerator) and some treats for passagemaking. We don't stock the boat this way with the expectation of not seeing a supermarket for a week, but simply as a convenience if we feel like anchoring off for a few days, or don't feel like walking to the shop in the rain.

When moving countries, we do pay a little more attention to provisioning. There may be higher taxes on certain goods that can create price differences worth noting. A good example is filling your boat with diesel before leaving Ireland or the UK for France, or indeed filling your boat with wine if you're coming the other way! Money aside, it may be that there are particular treats that you've come to enjoy in one country that are not available in the next. For us, we do make great use of the humble baked bean in tomato sauce, a tricky thing to find on continental Europe but a useful form of currency among British and Irish cruisers. In France, we found a particular brand of canned ravioli to be very tasty; it came in a can large enough to satisfy us all on the occasion of a late-night arrival.

For those setting out, I wouldn't get too caught up in it. Chances are you will spend your first month cruising in familiar lands (at least you should), and by the time you venture to the more remote parts of the world, you'll know your personal needs better than any book can explain. Enjoy the whole journey, the food, the culture and the time, not just the travel.

11

Education on board

M One of the major considerations when cruising as
a family, especially one that begins their cruising life
with a younger child or children, is education. Luke
and Ella were 11 when we first revealed that we were
heading off to cruise the world and the first question
I got from friends and family was, 'Where will the
children go to school?' My stock response? They'd be
educated on board. In the interests of full disclosure,
Leonard and I are in a somewhat enviable position
because we are qualified teachers and between us we
have approximately 30 years' experience educating
teenagers. For me, cruising the world as a family was
made possible because we were prepared to take on
the responsibility of educating our children. This may
sound like an ideal situation, but Luke and Ella probably
experience this as a blessing and a curse in equal measure.
Having said that, even if you don't have a background in
education, home schooling is not as daunting as people
think, and this chapter encourages would-be cruisers to
examine how they might take on educating their own
children.

Luke and Ella attended mainstream primary school in our area before we left Ireland. I was very happy with the education they received there – like all children they had their ups and downs but that's life. I had already considered home schooling them when they were just starting school, but I was parenting alone at the time and needed to work to support us, making the option a non-starter.

Parental worries

Parents are filled with anxieties about taking children out of school and 'ruining their futures' in order to live out their own dream. I know this because I am one of those parents. They are fearful that their life choices will damage their child's prospects in some way. I think that is a reasonable fear, for we cannot know one way or the other. However, my research prior to departure indicated that children educated on board are just as well-educated and well-adjusted as their peers on land. That was good enough for me.

As parents, we are the primary educators of our children; it is from us that they learn language skills, appropriate behaviour and socialisation skills. This teaching and learning happens organically, usually without much thought. But the older our children get, the less we feel we know and can teach them, hence the evolution of schooling. However, home schooling is simply the process of overseeing your child's education in person, and there are endless resources to help you.

Education in all its forms

I wish to define formal education, non-formal education and informal education, as it may help to clarify how you will proceed as an educator while you follow your liveaboard dream. The definitions I use throughout this chapter are taken from the Organisation for Economic Co-operation and Development (OECD), which has 36 member countries, each of which is committed to developing good practice and policy in areas that stimulate economic progress and world trade. Education falls into this category. I have chosen the OECD definitions because, as with the organisation itself, they have an international dimension and were developed in a co-operative manner. Furthermore, they haven't arisen from an 'educational purist's' point of view, giving them a distinct advantage.

Formal education

Formal education is classroom-based learning delivered by a trained teacher following an agreed curriculum and meeting agreed educational standards. This education results in certification, usually following examination.

Non-formal learning

Non-formal learning includes various structured learning situations that do not have a curriculum or accreditation associated with it. The learner's objective may be to increase skills and knowledge, as well as experience the emotional awards associated with an increased love of a particular subject or passion for learning. This would fit with learning and teaching in an organisation such as the Scouts, for example.

Informal education

Informal education is the learning that takes place outside of a structured curriculum. It encompasses student interests but is not limited to the classroom setting and often takes place at community-based programmes and/or after-school clubs, and in libraries or museums. It works through conversation, and the exploration and enlargement of experience.

It is likely that you will engage in all three types of education on board. However, the type that causes most concern for parents is probably formal education, so let us now consider the issues it raises and how you can address them.

Embracing home schooling

Schooling becomes an issue for liveaboards when they travel with their children and therefore cannot attend school in the same way as land-based children. For this reason, parents find themselves facing the question of how they will provide for their children's education. First, as with all other aspects of boat life, I suggest you do extensive research well in advance of your departure date. There are many excellent websites and social media locations online that provide insight and useful advice about how to proceed with home schooling. In addition, I recommend that, as parents, you discuss the desired outcome/s for your child/ren regarding education because this affects how you proceed. At this point, most average parents have a bit of a panic attack!

There are a variety of reasons why parents may be afraid of becoming their child's educator. Maybe some feel that they did not achieve at school and are poor role models. Perhaps they are anxious about their own standard of education or their ability to teach to specific exam requirements. They may feel they don't know where to begin, or fear their kids will not take them seriously. Many people see teaching as beyond their capabilities. Whatever the reason, each is real and valid. However, if you are to persist with your dream and you have children of school-going age, you will need to face these fears and embrace home schooling. This is actually a positive thing; the reason your children won't be attending mainstream schooling is because you are pursuing an alternative lifestyle. Most people who boat-school do so in a positive frame of mind, and that is a good place to start.

Asking the right questions

In today's world, there is an endless amount of information. This doesn't necessarily make things easier and it can often mean that knowing where to begin becomes a little overwhelming. Where does one start when planning their child's education? It's useful to break this question down into more manageable chunks, so let us begin with the practical aspects.

Legal status of home schooling

Before going any further, you must first consider the following questions.

1. What is the legal situation with regard to home schooling in your home country?
2. If it is illegal, how do you intend to manage that situation and avoid prosecution?
3. If it is legal, then what is the procedure?
   a. Is there a regulating authority with which you need to register your child?
   b. Are there requirements regarding record-keeping and home visits?
   c. Are you required to follow a prescribed curriculum?
   d. Is your child required to undergo standardised testing?
   e. Is your child required to undertake state examinations?
   f. How might you manage state examinations?
4. What is the situation with regard to home schooling in the countries you intend to visit? Are you required to comply with these regulations?

It may surprise you to know that there is a considerable variation internationally regarding parents being the providers of education for their children.

International variations regarding home schooling

The European Union

- There is general consensus that attending a state-funded school is compulsory between the ages of 6 and 16 years.

- However, most states in the European Union have protected the right of parents to educate their children outside of this system. Usually this protection is in the form of an amendment to the state's national education act.

- No such amendment exists in either Spain or Germany and therefore home schooling is illicit in the former and illegal in the latter. The German government actively pursues parents who home school in the courts and at the time of writing there are several such court cases in progress. The situation is less clear in Spain.

- Many EU states, such as Ireland, require parents of home-schooled children to register with the education authorities. These authorities conduct home visits and assessments to establish that the child/ren is/are being educated and not sent out to work. However, the authorities do not direct curriculum or require assessment.

- Some states, such as France, protect the rights of parents to home school but are directive about the curriculum pursued and rigorously monitor the education provided.

- The UK has, at present, the most liberal and unstructured approach to home schooling in the EU. Currently, legislation is being drafted for consideration in the House of Commons to change this, but please note that given Brexit, this too might of course be subject to change.

- Except for France, there is no evidence of the requirement to participate in the state examination system when a child is home schooled. France also requires home-schooled children to participate in standardised testing.

The USA

- Home schooling has been legal in all 50 states since 1993.
- Approximately two million students in the USA are home schooled at present.
- The US Supreme Court has ruled 'that parents have the fundamental right to direct the education of their children'.
- Considerable differences exist from state to state regarding the directions for curriculum, standard testing and even registering a child as home schooled. Legal cases are not uncommon.

Canada

- It is compulsory to attend school in Canada between the ages of 5 and 18, depending on where you live.
- There are ten states and three territories in Canada. The difference between a state and a territory is the structure of the governance; however, all recognise the right of parents to home school.
- There is a significant difference in the requirements regarding registering as a home schooler, submitting school-work plans and participation in standardised testing from state to state.
- Some states in Canada provide funding to home-schooling parents.
- There is a move away from faith-based home schooling to more mainstream home schooling.

Australia

- It is compulsory to engage in education in Australia between the ages of 6 and 16.
- Australia has six states and two territories, and each has its own education act.
- Home schooling is legal in all states and territories.
- Parents who home school are required to register their children with the school registration authority in their home state and have their curriculum inspected.
- Australia has a system of government-regulated distance-learning schools, through which a child

registers to participate in the government-provided curriculum but they do not physically attend. The child and his/her family have access to school resources and trained teachers. This requires the student to follow the curriculum outlined in a developmental way through the model of distance learning. The school is responsible for the education outcomes.

How to proceed

As you have probably worked out by now, there is considerable work to do before you can embrace home schooling. If your child already attended mainstream school, you will know that schools organise a considerable amount in the provision of education, and it may seem like an impossible task right now. However, home schooling is perfectly doable – in addition, you have the advantage of having a smaller and more interesting classroom! When it comes to preparation, a great place to start is *Finding Your Element*, by Ken Robinson.

Here are some other steps to take once you've undergone the initial research into home schooling.

Find a support group

One of the most difficult things about home schooling is feeling alone. In Ireland, 750 children are currently registered as home schooled, and two of them live with me! Finding a support group will help you to refine your thinking and grow in confidence as a home schooler. Living on a boat, your support group may be online, but there are fabulous ones available, so seek them out.

Take your time

I hear lots of talk about the curriculum, and what you should follow, and how you get the resources, and is it any good... It's too soon for all that yet! If you're new to living on a boat and you are already adapting to this new way of life, that is enough to be going on with. Give yourself time to adjust and spend time getting to know your kids. Give your kids time to get used to the freedom of life on a boat and throw off the shackles of school.

Create space and routine

Once you are ready to begin schooling, you can start by setting a routine and choosing a space for lessons. This obviously presents quite a challenge in a boat, but I am a firm believer in creating time first – the joy of home schooling is getting to spend so much time with your children. If you create a routine it will ease all of you into the transition of life on board and provide your child/ren with a sense of security.

Space is a whole other ball game. Using the salon table works; it means you have to tidy away after work, but this is only problematic if you are engaged in project work. Public spaces in proximity to your boat are a godsend.

Libraries are the obvious ones but we have also used the beach, picnic tables, parks – anywhere you can sit comfortably and work.

What are your goals?

It is important to consider what you would like your child/ren to achieve through home schooling. This will also give a focus to the learning. Do you want your teenager to sit state examinations in your home country? Is he/she seeking a place in university? Is he/she a gifted musician and seeking a place in a prestigious music school? Perhaps he/she is looking to run a business? Whatever your and your child's goals, this will impact on how you home school. If you are preparing a child for reception or preschool, then you have a whole other agenda, and so does your child.

What are your child's strengths?

One of the most important variables to consider is, of course, your child. What do you know about how your child learns? Does he/she need to see and hear things in order to engage? Is it important to them to experience the learning or build on what they know already? Do tests freak them out? Does he/she have a passion for art, music, sport, chess, making, baking or reading? Take the time to find your child's strength and passion, and to help them find it too, along with their preferred way of learning. Do not be afraid to challenge your child/ren – they will meet the challenge.

Choose a curriculum

Deciding what curriculum you will follow can be a bit of a minefield because there are so many variables at play. First, there are hundreds of people in the business of supplying curricula, so it is a difficult one to negotiate. Second, unless you are a teacher you will probably feel intimidated by the choice. My advice is to take it easy; if you go online to the government website of your country or state and find the education section, there will be a link to curriculum guidelines for each age group (see the Useful Resources on pages 336, where I have included several websites as a guide to get your started). I advise talking to a teacher you know, perhaps your child's current teacher, about suitable resources to meet the requirements of your chosen curriculum.

Get online

I cannot stress enough how many excellent home-school sites there are online. Trawl through them until you find one that fits with your ideals. I personally like www.thecanadianhomeschooler.com, as it is clear, secular and run by experienced educators. It also addresses the question of pedagogy, which is the discipline that deals with the theory and practice of teaching and how both influence student learning. This may be useful information for you or it may not – you decide.

Keep a record

Be sure to keep samples of the work your child produces and to date it. Find a simple boat-friendly way to do this.

When you are saving space, it is useful to catalogue by photograph or video, but I like to keep some original material, too.

Mix it up!
Formal, informal, fun, art, visits to museums, landmarks or local schools, hang-outs with locals – the options for education on the move are literally endless. Listen to your kids, ignore your kids, reflect a little on what you are learning yourself. Teach them to cook and bake and make and sew, to change oil, identify wildlife and to be kind. Have them listen to the news and talk about politics, and become socially aware and responsible. Let them hang out with other kids and make beach fires and cook what they catch. Teach them the value of friendship and to be free and safe, and most of all teach them the joy of spending time with people they might never otherwise encounter.

The pros and cons of home schooling for liveaboards

Home schooling is an alternative choice, there is no doubt, but statistics show that it is on the rise internationally. Home schooling on a boat brings a whole new dimension! Therefore, it may be useful to consider both the pros and the cons before deciding if this is for you.

Pros of home schooling

- Home schooling allows you to spend more time with your children and gain first-hand experience of their learning.
- It can be a positive challenge for both you as a parent and your children. You have the pleasure of seeing your children grow in independence and independent thought (although there is a risk that they may use it to challenge you!).
- Home schooling on a boat allows for tremendous freedom on several levels. You are freed from land life, but you have the added freedom to design learning events that allow your child to grow and develop. You also have the freedom to witness their development.
- You get to assume responsibility for your child's education. While this can sometimes be onerous, it can also be extremely satisfying.
- You work hard as a home educator, thereby stretching your own learning capacity and increasing your knowledge.
- There is the freedom for creativity.
- Your child will constantly evolve as a learner as they become their own educator and you, too, evolve as a learner as well as an educator.

Cons of home schooling

- There is an adjustment period when your children challenge your authority as an educator.
- You will challenge your status as a legitimate educator of your children.
- Your children will miss some of the social aspects of mainstream school.
- Some children will miss the competitive aspect of the mainstream classroom.
- You will likely be perceived as eccentric and alternative as a result of the choices you have made, and so will your children.
- Your child's route to university will be longer and it will be more difficult to prove his/her standard of education.
- Your child may not participate in state examinations.
- You may experience resistance from family and friends.

These are the legitimate pros and cons of home schooling but there is probably an equally long list for mainstream education. Liveaboards also find many solutions to educating their children, including sending them to local schools when they berth up or running an informal classroom in a marina. There are as many models as there are families. Usually the process of education when families are underway is different to when at anchor or moored. But remember, children are remarkably resilient; they'll grow and develop despite how we parent them. Your only job as a parent is to provide opportunities for your child to learn and grow in freedom and safety.

Home schooling on Faoin Spéir

It is not overstating the fact to say becoming liveaboards has been a steep learning curve for each one of us. But we think of education as a life-long process on board *Faoin Spéir*, and every day presents many opportunities for learning and teaching.

In terms of formal education, we are working on the Irish curriculum as outlined by the Irish Department of Education and Skills. If the children complete state examinations, and I am yet to make a decision either way, it will probably be the Irish state exams. Because they have attended primary school in Ireland, one of the implications for taking state exams is the requirement to study the Irish language. The formal system of education in Ireland is broken down into primary school (ages 5 to 13) and secondary school (ages 13 to 18). There are two state exams in secondary school: the Junior Certificate and the Leaving Certificate. The Leaving Certificate and the Matriculation Examination are computed independently for entrance into an Irish university, college or other third-level institute.

Formal education means lessons together every morning, Monday to Saturday from 9am to 11am. We tried many variations and this routine ended up working out best for us, for a number of reasons: everyone is fresher;

it allows time to complete assignments and project work independently; it frees up the afternoon for individual pursuits or family trips; Luke and Ella have no access to their phones during this period of the day, as they are charging.

A side note on mobile phone usage

Our solar panels provide limited electricity. Also, we do not want Luke and Ella to spend their entire lives with their noses stuck to their screens. So, when we first moved on board we decided as a family that two hours was sufficient time to charge one's phone. The children are granted this charging period every day and when it runs out, there is no recharging so no more phone for the day. They must be up and out of bed to charge their phone and they may begin charging earlier than 9am if they wish, but they have to unplug at 11am. They are not allowed to charge or take their phones into their own cabins. They both consider this period up to 11am as dead time anyway, so they might as well be engaged in learning, as it's less boring!

Everyone we meet has an opinion on this charging system, mostly encouraging Luke and Ella to find ways around it. But what we do works. The children have become responsible for their own phone usage. They have learned to save their phone time for contacting friends as a priority and only use it for watching videos on YouTube when all communication is exhausted. It also ensures that everyone is up early and ready to start the day.

For the first few months of living on board, our approach to schooling was based around figuring out what the children were capable of in terms of academic basics. In our case, this is Irish, English and maths. We were also interested in teaching them a new set of skills, including critical thinking, learning to ask the right

Lessons happen inside and out.

questions, and learning how to research with and evaluate sources. At first the children were deeply frustrated by our approach, because they were learning something new and had little opportunity to show how good they were. In fact, they were doing well because the point was that they were becoming motivated by their own learning. However, if I were to do it all again, I might have left them to their own devices at first, to see what direction they might take (although I suspect it would have led to hours and hours of video games − or at least until the electricity ran out!).

Leonard and I share the input. Leonard covers maths and art. I cover Irish, English, French, science, history, geography, home economics and creative thinking. I consider formal lessons essential to maintaining a routine and developing the mind. Over and above formal education, Luke and Ella read, take part in photography and film-making, swim most days and kayak and fish when the weather allows. So far we do not follow the school holiday calendar, as we believe that is essential to keep the momentum for learning going.

Informal education

Informal education takes many forms, but we are firm believers in taking every possible opportunity to learn and teach, although I imagine this makes us quite unbearable! Mealtimes are a great chance for informal learning because there is usually scope for some excellent chat. Last night at dinner, for example, Luke got the ball rolling with his question, 'What makes you from a particular place?' The art of argument, of making your point and being able to back it up logically, is highly prized on our boat.

Both children are now able to do the laundry – they load it and wash it, dry it, fold it neatly and put it in their rooms. They can cook simple meals and actively choose new food and flavours when the opportunity presents. They also complete chores in the boat, such as tidying, fetching water, washing up and keeping their rooms tidy. They are both capable of finding their way around the London Underground and planning routes to and from airports. In addition, they have a working knowledge of sailing and reading charts. I think as boat kids go they are average. All in all I am very happy with their education on board *Faoin Spéir*.

I would hate you to feel like it was all rosy in the garden though because it is not – they are teenagers after all, so let's not kid ourselves. I get sass on a regular basis. Though both have settled into cruising life, they miss their friends and school, and their cousins and hanging out at home. Because of this emotional turmoil, sometimes we have outbursts of aggression and plain bad temper. These also are opportunities for learning for all of us. Emotional regulation is an essential life skill and being able to practise it on the boat makes for an easier life for everyone. So, this means calling out behaviour and attitude when it happens, exploring what is going on and looking for alternative approaches. As I say, we are very popular! However, this is one of the advantages of educating on board; there is time to address issues and we are personally invested in improving behaviour.

A word on higher education

Without doubt, the most straightforward way to satisfy the necessary prerequisites for the purposes of a college application is for your children to attend a formal school setting. Schools are genuine experts at ensuring all of the formalities that go along with such applications are satisfied. But with a little organising, the same formalities can be achieved from anywhere in the world.

The first thing to do is decide which exam set you would like to follow and as every country has its own set, it would be foolish to try to include all of these here. The most common for English-speaking Europeans are the British A-levels and, to a lesser extent, the Irish Leaving Certificate. Both can be completed without the need to register with a school, although it is necessary to register with a specific exam centre. For A-levels in particular there are a huge amount of resources available to support distance learning, with many providers offering unlimited tutor contact via email and video calls. I have made a list of some of these providers in the Useful Resources section (pages 342–343), and having had direct experience and contact with several of these providers, I've found them to be very helpful and informative.

Learning for all

Leonard and I are both self-confessed nerds – probably have been most of our lives – but learning holds endless wonder for us. As liveaboards we are constantly looking for good sources of education that do not cost an arm and a leg, or preferably cost nothing. We have come up with some ingenious sources.

Libraries

First, libraries are among the best sources for learning around the world. Furthermore, they are free, for the most part, as long as you can provide an address. Now, that could be a problem for most liveaboards, but we have found librarians to be possibly the most helpful civil servants of all. Honesty is always the best policy and we have found that if you tell people your story they are more than willing to help. So smile and ask, and if they are unable to help, be gracious anyway – it costs nothing!

Online courses

It goes without saying that there is a wealth of information online. Yes, I know that nowadays all you have to do is 'Google' and the answer is there, but there are many well-founded sources of education worth mentioning. Open University is a market-leader of correspondence courses, and all their services – courses, exams, access to trained teachers and tutors – are now available online. But what many don't know is that Open University also offers free online courses, over a thousand of them. There are a huge variety of courses on offer and the standard is very high. I've found them to be exceptionally well-organised and presented, with courses to suit all abilities and interests.

Field trips

Our ongoing education has expanded at a great rate through visiting museums and galleries, parks and monuments, and no end of other fascinating sites and cities. As a result of our visiting so many places of historic interest, Leonard has rekindled his interest in history and philosophy and by association he has nudged me into reading up on some material I had forgotten due to old age and lack of use! Yes, it is a bit indulgent, but it is only indulgent because we have created this time for learning and education. Expanding our own knowledge can only be beneficial to the children and, in addition, we are continually modelling the value of learning all the time, and that is priceless as far as I am concerned.

Babies and toddlers

I recognise that if you are cruising with a small child or baby, your education needs are very different. There are many avenues to consider and among them is letting your child attend local schools. I know of several cruisers who educate their children with huge satisfaction in this way. I also know of situations where several cruisers come together and take responsibility for different aspects of education. There are as many options as people and children.

Again, may I recommend www.thecanadianhome schooler.com. It outlines the skills you should be trying to foster in your preschooler in order to ready them for reception, and some suggestions on how to achieve this. In a nutshell, research, read and reflect on what you want for your child and then make it happen. Have faith in yourself.

12

Letting go psychologically

Choosing an alternative lifestyle, as we have, is not all that difficult. The process of changing your life around to embrace the new lifestyle, now that is a whole other story. We had done lots of planning and research and spoke to people who had gone before us, but in truth, the real impact only fully hits you when you have untied the lines and made the move. My friends and family had said things to me like, 'How will you cope with two teenagers in a confined space?', 'Will you not grow tired of each other, spending so much time together?', and, my personal favourite, 'How will you manage without a garden shed to banish him to when you fight?' I dismissed all these questions thinking that I could manage whatever comes along. Oh my god, how wrong was I!

I had read many books that covered moving on board from a practical point of view. Now I know why none of those books had said anything about the emotional rollercoaster that is transitioning to living on board and sailing away. It's probably for the same reasons that very few women talk about the excruciating pain of childbirth.

First, nobody would have a baby if they knew how difficult childbirth can be, and second, when you have your baby and fall in love with its little body and soul you forget the pain you endured. But luckily for you I have not forgotten the pain of childbirth and I am prepared to share it in technicolour!

The transition

As a couple, we often talked about our dream of moving on to a sailboat and sailing around the world. When most people hear that they come back with, 'Oh you lucky things, living the dream'. Most people think that we *are* living the dream, so how could there be anything to transition into – how could there be sadness or loneliness or any other negative emotions?

For the first few weeks we lived on board I felt completely lost. I felt as if I knew nothing of who I was or who I had become in the years before that. Does this sound a little unhinged? It sounds crazy to me, too, but that is how it was in reality. I was no longer a teacher, a counsellor, a friend, sister or neighbour. I knew nothing about sailing. I could not sail. I followed instructions and I helped when asked. That was my contribution to the crew. I was, of course, a mother and a partner, but I was so overwhelmed by fear sometimes that I forgot this. Leonard, who is the sailor on our boat, did not have time or space to consider my terror, so I had to live with it. After I had prepared food and fed everybody I would sit in the galley and cry.

Why was I crying? I was terrified we were all going to die, I was going to die and be responsible for killing my children too! Leonard? I did not feel responsible for killing him; he had made his own decision. Let him die! But I had dragged my two innocent children kicking and screaming into this alternative lifestyle and now we were going to die! In more lucid moments I knew this was unlikely to happen, but the underlying terror pervaded every sinew of my body for most of the first six weeks after we left Ireland.

So why didn't I go home, just give up and go home?! I really don't know. Actually, that's not true, I do know: I didn't give up because I believe in challenging myself and working through the fear and not giving in to it. I didn't give up because I knew that if I went home, Leonard would go on without me and that would probably be the end of our relationship, and I love him and I want to live my life with him. I didn't give up because I had worked hard to get this far and I didn't want to falter at the first hurdle. I didn't give up because how can I teach my children to face their fears if I cannot model facing my own? How could I tell them that no feeling, no matter how strong, lasts forever? But I was tense and sharp, constantly barking at people and unpleasant to be around during the first sailing season.

So what did I do? I discussed my feelings with Leonard when we were in port and had the time to do so. I reflected and wrote about the process of what I was experiencing. I had no idea whatsoever what was involved in living this alternative lifestyle. In fact, living it poses massive challenges. I had presumed that all my old skills and abilities would be useful and help me to manage the challenges. Some of them were indeed useful, but not all.

The transition process took a long time. First, I had to let go of expectations. I learned to accept that 'the dream' is often the mundane in a different location.

Dealing with disbelief

When most people think of leaving family and friends they have one of two reactions: loneliness or relief. Maybe that is a bit extreme and there is a third possibility, which is anything along this spectrum. Living on board a sailboat and sailing the world definitely calls for letting go of family and friends and redefining your support network based on connectivity rather than physical presence or geographical state. We began this process quite a while before we actually moved on board by outlining our plan to our children and close friends and family. The response was almost universal disbelief, incredulity and, in some cases, active discouragement. Most people flat out refused to believe us at all, with more than a few describing it as 'far-fetched'.

It can be very difficult to keep your dream alive and focus on your goals and plans in the face of such resistance. So how did we manage it? We kept on talking about it in a real way and we informed people of the steps we were taking to make our plans concrete. You will already have read how we acquired our boat, and you also know that for two years after we purchased *Faoin Spéir* and before we moved her to the sea, she leaned up against our garden shed and became a landmark for the entire neighbourhood. But still people did not believe our plan to move on board and sail away. We answered all questions with openness and sincerity and confessed our ignorance when we did not have answers. I am sure we sounded naive – we were naive – but we were never defensive or arrogant. Our bottom line in reassurance was and continues to be that we do not wish to do anything to endanger our home or our family, so when we sail, we err on the side of caution – always.

I think the denial about our leaving came from a few different sources. Family and friends love us and rely on us for comfort and support, and they did not want this to end. There is a belief that other people embrace this kind of adventure, not the likes of us nor the people we know. There was – and continues to be – a certain amount of anxiety that we would come a cropper and die as a result of sailing on the high seas or encountering pirates. There is the loneliness caused by our departure, and most people in modern society avoid loneliness like the plague. Family and friends and indeed we, the crew of *Faoin Spéir*, struggled with a fundamental change in the nature of our relationships and this was scary for everybody. There was a fear that we would grow apart.

There is a big responsibility in being the ones to cause such huge turmoil for those we love, for 'no good reason'.

Ireland has a long history of immigration, of people having to leave the country to find work in order to become financially solvent. It's usually accompanied by bitter regret, a feeling that you are forced to go and a longing for the old country. Here I reference the huge library of song, story and poetry that exists on this very topic, very little of which is happy! We had no terms of reference for leaving freely to pursue adventure of one's own accord. Therefore, it was very difficult to explain that this was an occasion of happiness and not of sorrow, especially as our own feelings on the subject were very mixed.

Loss and loneliness

Luke and Ella were sad at the loss of their close friends and cousins. They were very regretful about not entering into secondary school and sharing that experience with classmates they had known and experienced their education with since preschool.

I had mixed feelings too, with sadness at leaving family behind, but not as much sadness as I felt leaving behind clients of our theatre company and my clients at my counselling practice. I think for me this loss was about the fact that I knew family would stay connected, but that this would not be possible – or even appropriate in some cases – for clients.

Leonard was positive and excited and showed no sadness at all, that is until he came face to face with separating from his son, and then it was a whole other

212

story. His grief was palpable. It all seemed so final at the point of departure, but of course the reality of the age of budget airlines means that we can make return visits or entertain guests on a regular basis. It would be a rare occurrence if more than a month passed without a visit in one direction or the other.

So how did we manage the separation from family and friends once it became apparent that we were actually leaving and following our dream? We spent time with them and we talked and talked and talked. We listened to people's concerns and we tried to address them, and when we could not, we were honest about that. That may seem very little and very obvious but at a time when we were up to our eyeballs working on the boat, closing down our business and emptying our house, taking the time to spend time with our family and friends was a huge deal. But we never failed to do so. Our priority was people and sharing with them what was happening for us. We never gave false assurances or made promises or tried to make people's sadness go away. Rather, we tried to honour our plans and help people understand what we were doing and why. Of course we also had several 'going away' parties, wonderful occasions where we chatted and danced and sang and drank and had lots of fun with our family and friends. At these parties we handed out our *Faoin Spéir* cards with details of our website (www.FaoinSpeir.com), YouTube channel and Twitter page (@FaoinSpéirYacht), so that people could follow our story and get the most up-to-date information about our travels.

Facebook has proved to be a wonderful tool for helping friends and family to keep in touch, too. I had resisted this option for many years due to my fear of social media. Through my work I had seen social media sites used as tools of abuse and misinformation, and I had and continue to have a mistrust of the false images they portray. However, I do feel social media has its uses, and telling the story of our adventure to family and friends is one such advantage.

So we continue to have a support network and feel connected to family and friends, it's just not in the flesh but in the virtual realm. For now, that is working pretty well. We are also very lucky to have made some good friends on our journey, other liveaboards who share our dream and have embraced us with warmth and openness, and regularly invite us to dinner.

No Garden Shed

Whenever we spoke of heading off to live on *Faoin Spéir*, people were full of awe and wonder that we would all live together in such a tiny space. But one of the main questions and 'with no garden shed'. I had one friend in particular who continually asked how we would manage without one. I was genuinely puzzled by the question, until one day I explained that we wouldn't have a garden so we wouldn't need a garden shed! My friend looked at me in utter amazement and said, 'But where will Leonard disappear to when you have a fight and you're not talking?' I finally got the concept of a garden shed and the obvious disadvantage of not having one as a kind of safety valve. And in that one sentence I began to realise the seriousness of living in such a small space with one other adult and two teenagers, and I had a fleeting panic attack. It lasted three seconds and then my optimism kicked in and I thought, 'Ahh, we'll be fine.' Sweet mother of the Divine Lord, what was I thinking?

I do not mean that in a mean or spiteful way; what I actually mean is what was I thinking?! Before we left we had done copious amounts of research, we had read serious volumes and talked to very experienced and practical cruisers. But now that I think about it, nobody had talked much about the struggles of a relationship in a confined space and being separated from your tribe, your home and everything you know. The one thing I had heard was that usually people who live the long-term cruising life do so because they want to spend more time together and have good, strong relationships to start with, so all is well. Upon reflection I should have seen that as an acknowledgement that a good, strong relationship was needed. This may very well be true, but it doesn't make things any easier. I would have said that Leonard and I had a very strong and close relationship but still, the first few months were incredibly tough. I am going to outline exactly why that was as far as I understand it.

When Leonard asked me if I would sail around the world with him, I had no clue what that meant – I have even less of a clue now! I have always wanted to travel to new destinations and live there for a while and set down roots, really get to know the place, buy bread and milk, go to church to see what it's really like to be a citizen of the place. Leonard's proposal appealed to the wanderlust in my soul. However, I did not sail at that point and I think I had rarely been on a sailboat either.

Nonetheless, we made our plan, bought our boat, got it in the water and we became full-time cruisers. It was

Before we even had a boat, we thought we would start at the
Prime Meridian in Greenwich.

216

a bit of a whirlwind. Looking back on it now, I think I found it all a bit unbelievable. I suspect I was carried along with my head in the sand.

Leonard was very practical and did all the work on the boat, the renovation and the physical work. I kept the finances flowing and prepared in other ways, like through reading and talking. However, in truth, I embraced a plan that was Leonard's and moved forwards with it. I am not sure how much of it I embraced or personalised. This became an issue for me and our relationship when we left Ireland and became full-time liveaboards. The tensions began to set in and boy, did I long for a garden shed!

Whose dream is it anyway?

Upon reflection I have some understanding of what went on for me at the time and I am going to share it, for what it's worth. The process of becoming full-time cruisers is a complex one. If both people in the partnership share the dream equally then it is straightforward and you can both actively pursue said dream. In my experience, the idea comes from one person in a partnership; the other person considers it and either accepts or rejects it. In the case of either response, both partners have considerable work to do to sustain the relationship. If the proposal is rejected, then where does that dream go and what are the implications for the future of the relationship? There is also the scenario where one partner does not want to become a cruiser but they pretend they want it, in the hope it will not happen. If this is your position, you probably have a whole lot of trouble in store. But if your partner agrees to follow the dream, there is still a whole lot of work to do to plan, implement and follow through.

This was the position I found myself in; I agreed to the dream and I still do, and I was carried along on the planning, implementing and follow-through. What I did not do, and it was a mistake on my part, was sit down and consider what the issues might be for *me*. I neither addressed them nor acknowledged them. Why did I not do this? I think there were many reasons. I was in a fairly new situation, uncharted waters, and I did not know the questions to ask at the time. I was afraid of facing the truth because I was afraid it might mean the end of our relationship. Leonard was pretty determined to go. I did quite like the excitement of it all and, yes, I recognise this is a contradiction but I think I have already established that I am a contradiction! As uncomfortable as it is to admit this, I think there was also a bit of 'Well, it is his dream and if I go ahead and support it then it gives me some power, something to have over him.' I know that's not nice, I know what it sounds like, but there is no point in writing about relationships and being dishonest. That is part of what went on for me and I am not proud of it, but there we are.

So I had all of these issues and emotions swirling around and, on top of that, I had no sailing experience, and every time we went out in the boat I was frightened, really frightened. I had no control or understanding of what was happening. Now, I know I am responsible for my own ignorance, but in my defence let me remind you that I was working full time while trying to close down our house and move on to a boat. I didn't have the time for preparation and training, and I was also resistant to it in some shape or form. I suspect my thinking, if I had voiced it, would have sounded like, 'Well, it's his damn dream, let him sail the bloody boat!'. In essence, what I did was disempower myself. I recognise that now, but at the time I was just trying to survive and get on with life.

As the weeks and months went by I found myself in the strangest place I had ever been in my life. I had no purpose. I had always worked and been employed in the caring professions, and without work and a home and roots I had no idea who I was. I did not recognise myself. My whole world was turned upside down.

In addition, I had Luke and Ella to consider. They were making a transition from land life to boat life and leaving behind friends and family and everything they had known their whole lives. It was a very tough time for them; they were lonely and tearful and a little resentful in the case of Luke and a lot resentful in the case of Ella. I was trying to support and encourage them as best I could. As adults we were in transition, too, leaving everything behind, but as adults we have life experience and the knowledge that goes with that. We have seen change several times, made fresh starts. We know we can survive and it will all work out. As a child, when it's your first time encountering such change, your whole world is being pulled out from under you and it is devastating. I had done the preparation and work to foster the transition for Luke and Ella but, still, it was tough for them.

I now know that I had not done the same level of preparation for myself. When we sailed away from Bere Island on that September morning, I was grieving for my friends, my family, my house, car, everything. I was not ready for this huge adventure. On that very morning, Leonard and I had a massive row as we packed the boat. We also had a silent raging row because we were on a marina in a very public place, where sound carries for miles. Have you ever been fuming and raging and had a silent fight? Suffice it to say, it made for a terribly miserable departure.

Hindsight is a wonderful thing and brings infinite wisdom. Our relationship has survived to date, but I don't feel in the least bit smug or satisfied about that, I can tell you. Relationships are hard work at the best of times and the first few years sailing was like having a new baby – the strain almost ended us. Add all of the above to the lack of privacy on a tiny boat where we don't even have a door on our cabin to slam and nowhere to go to have make-up sex. I don't wish to offend anyone or give too much information, but intimacy on a boat is difficult to achieve. Perhaps that is the issue. When I talk about intimacy I am not simply talking about sex, I am talking about the intimacy of closeness, trust, warmth, rapport, mutual support, solidarity and comradeship – all the things that go into making a good relationship. I would like to give more extensive consideration to the subject of relationships and long-term cruising but I'm reminded that, like the boat, space is also limited in this book.

Is cruising for me?

Consider the dream from the perspective of both people in the partnership before you begin planning or taking the steps to make it concrete. It is worth spending time on this, and I suggest starting by asking yourself the following questions:

- How do you envisage your life as a long-term cruiser?
- What is your greatest fear about cruising?
- What is your biggest hope for cruising?
- What do you personally stand to gain from cruising?
- What do you personally stand to lose from cruising?
- Do you have children/grandchildren/elderly parents?
- What strengths/weaknesses do you bring to cruising?
- What strengths/weaknesses does your partner bring to cruising?
- Are you willing to embrace the cruising life or not?
- What happens to your relationship if either of you does not want to cruise?

Take as much time as you need to consider these questions individually. Write in your journal or diary, meditate or do whatever it is you like to do to get inside your mind. When you are both finished you should sit down and talk about your answers. I would also advise revisiting the questions several times throughout the project, that is if you decide to go ahead and become long-term cruisers. Either person in the relationship should be able to raise concerns or change their minds at any time. Relationships need work and honesty. Truthfulness is your bedrock when you undertake a huge project like this and you need to be constantly talking to each other, all the time.

13

Letting go practically

L If you have ever had to move house, then I'm sure you've stood in front of a stack of boxes wondering how you came to gather so much 'stuff'. It seems that no matter how large your living space, there is always a tendency to fill it. It's not usually a problem until the day comes when you are moving to a smaller space, like a boat.

Minimal living

In practical terms, there are very few things in your home that you actually need in a boat. Come to think of it, there are probably very few things in your home that you need *in your home*. Let's try a little experiment: are you sitting in a room in your home right now? If not, then try this the next time you are. Let's suppose you're sitting in the kitchen. Look at all the individual items in the kitchen, especially the ones you haven't touched in months. Perhaps they're hidden away at the back of a cupboard – that muffin tray you haven't used in years, or the smoothie maker you switched on for three days in January. All of these unused items can disappear from your life immediately without having any impact on your day-to-day. Even the cups and plates – how many people in your household? Four? Five? Then why do so many of us have 30 dinner plates scattered around the various cupboards?

OK, that's just the stuff you rarely, if ever use, gone. Now look at the items you *do* use more regularly, like the coffee maker, the microwave, and the toasted sandwich maker. You probably don't need any of these items to function day to day. Yes, they make life easier, but they also make life more complicated. What is the first thing you do when the microwave breaks? Probably take out your phone and do a stock check at your local appliance store. I would be the first to admit that in a domestic kitchen a microwave is very handy. It reduces waste, allows meals to be prepared and frozen, and is the quickest and cleanest way to make scrambled eggs or boil a mug of milk for hot chocolate. But on a boat, it's not quite as useful. Without leftovers, the number of times you use a microwave oven is greatly reduced. Now, if I want a mug of hot chocolate, I boil the milk in a saucepan, just like I used to before I ever owned a microwave. It's all about what you get used to; remember, one of the positives of living on a boat is having a little more time in your life for the simple things, like brewing fresh coffee in the morning. These days it takes me longer to brew a pot of coffee than it used to take me to make and drink two mugs. But the coffee tastes a hundred times better.

Faoin Spéir **super coffee**

Fortunately, Mary and I have grown to like our coffee the same way. This means that we can make a fresh pot of coffee, complete with sugar and milk, all in the same pot. This is ideal on a boat where instead of bringing sugar, milk, spoons, mugs and a pot to the cockpit, we have only two mugs and a pot. Makes sense, but the coffee had a tendency to be a little cooler than I would like, particularly out in the fresh air. The solution? Powdered milk! I can hear the gasps from those of my generation who may be remembering the mouldy tub of powdered milk, hiding, forgotten at the back of the cupboard of our childhood. But its modern equivalent is a far superior product. So, each morning on *Faoin Spéir*, we start our day with 1.5 litres of coffee made with three heaped tablespoons of ground coffee, 1.5 level tablespoons of sugar and three regular tablespoons of powdered milk. Add water that has boiled and cooled for a minute or so and there you have it, salvation in a pot.

Ⓜ Never mind what Leonard says; if you have stuff you want to bring and you can find space for it on your boat then you should bring it with you. What may seem silly to us may be your essential item. He is right about one thing, though. You will bring too much and be sorry. But I can tell you this, you will also find your level, and you'll find a way to offload all the stuff you don't need. In other words, don't worry too much about it.

I would caution against getting into needless arguments about what you bring. If you find yourself arguing about nitty-gritty details like this I suggest you make a cup of tea, sit down and give time to considering what is really going on.

Selling up

Between us, Leonard and I had very little worth selling. We did hold a dry run at a yard sale in the December before we set sail and it had some limited success. Our timing was poor but it was a useful exercise in that it put down another marker on our pathway to moving on board. We did intend at the time to have a yard sale on another date, but we left it too late to organise and so ended up not doing it. In the end we donated most of the leftover stuff to charity. In truth, we could have sold some of it but we were not prepared to waste precious time for the funds it might raise. We also donated books to schools and children's libraries, some stuff went to family and the remainder is in storage.

Luke and Ella did not want to sell their things or give them to charity. The things I am referring to here are toys, collections and other childhood favourites. I did not push disposing of these items because I recognised the necessity of choosing my battles. I was also feeling a little anxious about how difficult their transition was, and how emotionally fraught it was to say goodbye to their friends and classmates, so I wasn't going to argue over a bunch of plastic invested with all the emotions of a happy, stable childhood.

To let or not to let

If you own your home, then there are some important decisions to be made. The options are simple enough: sell it or keep it. Everyone's circumstances are different but broadly speaking, selling your home is likely to give the coffers a welcome boost before you head off. If you are selling, it really is best to do so at least six months in advance of the off. This allows you to focus on one major undertaking at a time. For many people, selling their home and moving on to the boat for a year before cruising allows for a period of reduced costs and thus an increased rate of saving before untying the lines.

My house in the south of Ireland is an old cottage. It stands on an acre and a half at the foot of the Galtee mountains in a beautiful, picturesque part of County Limerick. It is where Luke and Ella lived their entire lives, until we moved on to *Faoin Spéir*, and so I chose not to sell. Doing this presents two more options: whether or not to let the house. I was struggling to make the transition to boat life myself and had no idea what shape that would take, so I was not ready to let go of the house. It was July, and we decided not to let the house until the following spring, so that it would always be available if I wanted to return home for a visit, or even Christmas. At least, that was the plan.

In fact, what happened was we let the house sit idle for the summer, while the boat eventually became home to us. However, as you will read elsewhere in the book, our first departure for the Scilly Isles did not go as planned and we had to return to Ireland to do some repairs to the boat. In that period, I returned to the house, prepared it for rental and found a tenant. This created some comfort for us financially and generated a small, but steady, income during our first year aboard.

Letting your house does come with its own problems. It's a little like running a small business remotely. If there's a problem, you're not there in person to deal with it, so you will need to either employ an agent or depend on family or friends to tend to the task. If being a landlord/lady was never one of your ambitions, the host of conditions and red tape that must be satisfied prior to rental may present as a huge stress-inducing headache. After a year afloat, we found that we could sustain our new life without the need to have a tenant, and so we opted to discontinue letting.

The postman

Ⓛ All the books told us to cancel everything and inform all contacts of our change of address. We continue to receive mail at our old address, but if you do decide to give up a postal address, you'll need to consider a range of issues. For one, banks and other financial institutions simply do not recognise the idea that some people may not have a physical address. Their systems cannot handle it, so if you are not maintaining your old address then you will have to provide them with the address of a trusted friend or relative. However, with the advent of email and internet banking, it is possible to leave your old address on the bank account and request that all correspondence be sent via electronic means.

Traditionally, long-term cruisers would have mail and parcels sent to yacht clubs that were en route, and in our experience most marinas are happy to receive post for you if you plan on staying with them for a few days. But do call ahead to make sure they are expecting both the post and you.

A relatively new concept, which has become so convenient for the liveaboard cruiser that a liveaboard cruiser could have created it, is the virtual postal address. There are several companies engaged in this model (including global brands like Amazon), and each country has its own version, but they all operate in the same way.

Essentially, virtual postal addresses are secure lockers placed in convenient or accessible locations, such as supermarket car parks or train stations. You usually need to create an online account, to send and receive post, but it is quite straightforward after that. To send, you go online and fill in the package details and address. This generates a label that you apply to the package. When you take the package to the lockers, you scan the label and a locker opens. Then you place the package into the locker and the company takes it from there.

The recipient will receive a text or email with a pin number or barcode to be entered/scanned at the destination address, and a locker opens with the parcel inside. The real beauty of this is that the service is available all day, every day. Even better, it's not restricted to personal post; most online retailers (including chandlers) have an option to ship through one of these services.

Packing

There is no hard-and-fast rule about what to pack and what not to pack. I'm not talking about foulies, boots and emergency flares (the pyrotechnic type, not the fashionable 1960s pants), but rather the personal items that will make a boat feel like home. It's always a struggle to leave stuff behind – even if you have not opened the cover of your favourite book in two years, you'll still want to bring it with you. But you have to be tough. First, living on a boat is a busy affair. I wouldn't suggest that you pack a whole pile of equipment for new hobbies you think you're suddenly going to take up. The first year will actually be taken up with learning how to live on a boat and you'll hardly have any time for your old hobbies, let alone new ones. It is even hard to find time for fishing – fishing! So, knitting machines, easels and that box set that'll teach you 12 new languages should be left behind, unless these are things that you already do before you leave. There will be time enough in the future to take up new hobbies, just not in the first year.

Of course, you could bring extras, as most people do. You'll find your ideals shifting as you go, and every now and then you'll find a bin in which to dump the extras as you go. It is likely that the further you sail, the simpler you will wish your life to be. Personally, I didn't have much on land and so it was easy to pack for a life on the sea. I packed clothes. Otherwise, my packing consisted of tools and spare parts – nothing else personal except for books. I had many more books than a normal person should have, and there were some that I just had to bring. So Mary and I agreed that we could pack one plastic tote each of personal books, and another two of work-related books. Considering that I now see writing as my livelihood, I could argue that all of my books are work related!

(M) Packing is a nightmare. It caused me no end of grief and distress. Maybe I was tired and emotional at the time but it was hell. It is not the same as packing for your annual two-week holiday; this is packing up all your worldly goods and chattels, and moving everything you need for life, work, play, entertainment and study on to a small boat without any clue as to how that life will actually look.

So how did I decide what to bring? I started out by making a list of the spaces in the boat and the activities we needed to do, and from there decided what I thought we might need. There were some criteria: for example, priority was given to those things we needed for work and home schooling, such as electronic items. Each of us has a laptop, an e-reader and a mobile phone. Ella and I also have iPods, while the children and I brought our own Nintendo DS. Leonard has all manner of electric tools. We also carry a sewing machine and a printer with a built-in scanner for use as a photocopier. We have a smart TV on board and a Nintendo Wii.

Once I'd finished my list, I packed everything into bags, carried them to the boat and tried to fit them in. We were slightly hampered by the fact that the boat was not finished, so we didn't actually have anywhere to store our things. The level of clutter and disorganisation really challenged me. I was like a demented cow after giving birth! No disrespect to cows, but I was raw and frazzled and not in a good place. Funnily enough, it was not the downsizing and loss of all my modern conveniences and comforts that got to me; rather, it was the not being able to organise things the way I wanted in my new home. What a woman! I think growing up in the mid-60s and early 70s without running water and a bathroom in the house prepared me well for boat living, as did living in a convent with no washing machine in the 80s. However, we all have our breaking point, and mine is living in chaotic surroundings.

We have many books on board, more than any other boat I have visited. Leonard built space into the design specifically for them. We also trade books, buy them second-hand and swap them with other English-speaking liveaboards. We carry sailing and first aid books, almanacs and one cookbook, my precious dairy cookbook, which is a bit old-fashioned but it the best there is, in my opinion.

When we moved on board, we gave Ella and Luke a little bin, approximately 60cm x 30cm x 30cm, and told them they could fill it with personal items, which did not include books or writing materials or anything necessary for school. The only real stipulation was that they needed to be able to carry it on board themselves (I had to add this rule, otherwise Ella would have tried to bring her collection of plastic horses, and we'd then be looking at the weight of an alternative anchor!). In fact, the children both proved to be very sensible and brought a variety of items.

Ella packed her riding boots and helmet, some of her plastic horses and figurines, her bow and arrows, several cherished soft toys and photographs, and DVDs and games in addition to her favourite books. Luke brought his hurleys and sliotars (respectively, the stick and ball used in the Irish game of hurling), his rugby boots and ball and an old leather football, Buttons (his first ever teddy), some DVDs, books and his Manchester United memorabilia.

Leonard and I packed very little in terms of personal belongings. I brought my jewellery-making materials and tools and other art materials, but I consider that to be part of our money-making potential. Finally, as you know, we brought our sprung double mattress from home, which Leonard carried down to the boat by himself and which miraculously fitted through the hatch and on to our bed base, made especially for the purpose. It is super luxurious and comfortable.

Clothes

Clothes proved to be a bit of a thorny issue, which surprised me a little. We packed primarily for warm summer climates, as when we left Ireland our destination was the south of Spain. However, plans changed and we had to bring extra warm clothing. The other problem is having two teenagers who grew up with central heating and therefore had very little idea of what it means to add layers for keeping warm. They just didn't get the concept of putting on a few thin layers being a better option than wearing one thick, woolly layer. The other bit they didn't get was that clothes aren't just for fashion; sometimes they're for comfort, and at sea they are for comfort and heat. But they learned the hard way.

Christmas decorations

Among the items we decided to bring on board were the Christmas decorations from our house in Ireland. Now, it may seem daft to go to the bother of bringing Christmas decorations but there is method in my madness. Making the transition from home to sea is emotionally fraught enough as it is, and Christmas became a very contentious issue. It is rife with tradition and in our family, we had a very definite tradition. Every Christmas, for as long as Ella and Luke were around, my sister, Mairead, and her three children joined us for the holidays, while on the big day one or two others would come round for Christmas dinner.

Christmas on the boat raised lots of issues, as we had anticipated it might. First, we came under extreme pressure to return to Ireland for the festivities. There was a temptation to give in on our first Christmas, as we were very close in the UK and it would have been so easy. However, we made the decision to stay and celebrate it together on the boat and make some new memories. If we were to go home, it would set that expectation up for every year to come, and it would always be an issue. But now it will always be our choice. It was well worth the consideration given to packing to have our treasured decorations with us. I cannot fully explain how having them and a real tree helped to make our first Christmas on board one we will never forget.

14

Getting underway

For me, and as seems to be the case for those who have gone through it before me, the final few weeks before departure were a blur. Any effort to get work done was hampered by visits from well-wishers, and it was wonderful. When we got a call, it was a great excuse to stop the frantic running around and sit and chat with someone who invariably brought much-needed positive energy to the table. There was little time for anxiety. Being fearful or anxious doesn't change anything, so I focus on the task at hand and save the emotional stuff for later. I know in the moment it presents as though I haven't a care in the world, that I'm supremely confident about the whole endeavour, but that's not the case. It's simply that considering whether it will fail or succeed does not change the work needed to succeed.

A lot of people who know me see my approach as eternally optimistic and even naive. The truth is that, throughout the entire *Faoin Spéir* project I've been neither optimistic nor pessimistic. I've just carried on. When you set your sights on a grand adventure, and you figure out a way to make it happen, it's no longer a dream that you aspire to, it's a plan that you are following. And a dream requires hope, but a plan requires perseverance. Perseverance is in your own hands while hope is some uncontrollable wish or desire. So, when I'm working towards a goal, I follow the plan with perseverance. In the end, you have succeeded or not. If you have not, it's not that you've failed, but probably the cost of continuing has become too great and you had given as much as you were willing to make it work.

I guess such an adventure is a bit like an auction. You go as far as you are willing to go and if that's enough, then your goal has been achieved. But if the goal costs too much, you stop and recognise that you've tried as hard as you are willing to do. This doesn't mean that things won't change in the future and that you'll never try again. It just means now is not the time. But for us, it was our time.

Departure

It's hard to pinpoint the exact time and date of our departure on *Faoin Spéir* – was it when we left Bere Island, or when we set out from Ireland? For me, the second phase of the project began when we sailed off the pontoon in Bere Island with no intention of returning.

It was 13 September 2016. After four years of planning and daily input, we finally slipped the lines. I should mention here that September is definitely *not* a good time of year to be setting off. Most boats at our latitude were being taken out of the water for wintering, but due to all manner of events and reasons, September was our only opportunity that year – any later and we would've had to wait until late spring, which, for the record, is the correct time to set out.

Our destination that day was Schull, a beautiful little town in West Cork, with a wonderful natural harbour that gives shelter in all but the strongest southerlies. Looking back now, the seven-hour trip was nothing, but for a green skipper and crew, sailing around Ireland's most southerly headland was just the challenge we needed to boost our confidence in both the boat and its sailors. Not an hour out and we found ourselves motor-sailing into a short 2-metre chop that was being funnelled up Bantry Bay, in the middle of which the radio crackled to life. The Irish navy was trying to make contact with us, as part of a radio exercise. It was our first official use of the radio. Here we were, setting off on our 'adventure to everywhere', and although Mary had the VHF Radio Operators certificate and we had a Ships Radio Licence, we had never actually used the radio at sea.

The naval radio operator asked us the following information:

- The boat's name and registration number
- The Maritime Mobile Service Identity (MMSI) number, a unique nine-digit number, a bit like a mobile phone number, which is assigned to your boat's radio unit

- The owner's names
- The number of crew on board
- Our port of departure and intended destination.

We eventually escaped the bay and brought the sea and wind on to our beam as we rounded Sheep's Head. The swell was there but that short chop had subsided. We were sailing! We had left and we were sailing! At this point, if we never got any further than Schull, we had gone from not having a boat to living aboard a 12-metre sailboat and setting out with no planned end to the journey.

The leg between Sheep's and Mizen heads was a struggle for the crew, as the beam on seas made sitting difficult. The emotions probably didn't help either, I'm sure, but I felt elated. The sailing was great, we were making 6 knots, the sun was out and the boat was like an eager puppy chasing a toilet roll down a staircase.

Once around the Mizen, we turned east, and immediately the boat flattened out, the wind and seas working with *Faoin Spéir*, driving her eastwards. The cockpit, which had been a very quiet place for the previous three hours, was suddenly filled with chatter and smiles. The conditions hadn't changed but our orientation to them had, and it made a huge difference in terms of crew comfort. Soup and sandwiches made an appearance shortly thereafter, soon followed by dolphins. (When you're out on the boat, particularly when there are no other boats about, and dolphins appear, there is always a feeling of ease. It's as though they are looking out for you.)

With Schull in sight, we took in the sails and sought out the buoy that marked our home for the next few days. Few things show how far we have come as a crew as picking up a mooring, and even though we struggled to find our target buoy among the many others in the mooring field, our approach was calm, controlled and methodical.

Our mooring ball routine

We use the same routine every time we pick up a mooring ball. Mary takes the helm and lines up downwind or tide of the buoy. I am on the bow giving hand signals for left or right (arms outstretched). Luke is at the mast and Ella at the windscreen, relaying my instructions back to the helm. I might say 'Throttle back', followed by Luke, then Ella and finally Mary will throttle back. This works very well for us; there is no shouting and, with practice, everyone knows their place and what to expect. We use a similar approach when anchoring.

Tied up, kettle on, time to allow the delight of a safe and successful sail flood through our bodies. It was not the 35 nautical miles we covered but the first step in the many thousands more we hoped to cover.

That evening we completed our first transfer from boat to tender, our first row ashore, and our first night aboard on a swinging mooring. I'm sure there were dozens of other firsts but these were the important ones. These were the firsts that demonstrated to us that our dream for living aboard was within our capabilities. Of course, we had planned to practise all of these things before setting off in a 'shake-down cruise', but I wonder if that would have detracted from the sense of adventure. Perhaps I would've spent that first night having to remind myself this wasn't a two-week cruise that would end with a return to life on land. Maybe I wouldn't have enjoyed the true gravity of the position in which I found myself.

After a few days in Schull, we lined up another first. For me, and I think for many sailors, this one is a real bogeyman: night sailing. We decided to make life as easy as possible for ourselves and planned to sail from Schull to Kinsale (about 50 miles) overnight. It was not just any night; we selected a full moon and perfect weather. Casting off from the mooring with enough time to clear the rocks and islands surrounding Schull, we ensured we'd be clear of land before sunset. I was glad we did, as we met some very lumpy seas in the channels between the islands while trying to clear land. It was just as we turned eastwards that I looked over my shoulder to see the last sight of the sun until it appeared on the other horizon.

That first night was magical, nerve-wracking and satisfying all at once. We arrived into Kinsale ahead of schedule and in the dark. I know a lot of sailors, many of whom I would consider mentors, have said that they would rather stay out at sea until daybreak than make a new harbour under cover of darkness. However, although this was our first time arriving at Kinsale by boat, I had visited the town many times and had a sound understanding of the geography of the area. Were I not in possession of this knowledge, I probably would have entered the port in darkness regardless. It has since been our experience that navigation aids, such as lit buoys and marks, GPS and our electronic charts, make night entries to unfamiliar ports much easier than they would have been even 20 years ago.

Arriving to the shelter of Kinsale harbour after our first night passage was a relief. We had faced another hurdle in our very steep learning curve and succeeded in completing the task safely and without undue stress. Night passage: check.

We found ourselves in an area of the Irish coast closest to the Isles of Scilly off the south-west tip of the UK, 140 or so nautical miles south-east – open ocean, so to speak. We had a few more things to sort before making that giant leap, and so we took a trip up into Cork City, before making our way back out to the mouth of Cork Harbour to Crosshaven. It was from here that we would say goodbye to Ireland and thrust ourselves into the many more 'firsts' that lay ahead.

Our first emergency at sea

From Mary's journal: We set out from Cork on October 1st with a lot of excitement and hope, delighted to be finally getting underway on our first offshore excursion. We had some anxiety, being well aware that even with in-depth preparation there are variables outside of our control that could make life difficult for us. Accompanied by Ian Cunningham, a sailing friend and fellow liveaboard from the Isle of Wight, we left Crosshaven at 5.30am, long before sunrise, leaving the pontoon under sail in a gentle and quiet movement that has come to be Leonard's signature manoeuvre.

We negotiated the exit from Crosshaven in the dark by following the markers and buoys, and all was fine. Leaving the port of Cork, we encountered force 5 winds on the stern and an Atlantic swell of 3 metres, but *Faoin Spéir* is a sturdy boat, not afraid of a small Atlantic swell, and Leonard and Ian had her surfing those waves with ease and all three were having a ball.

As the sun rose we were anticipating a day of superb sailing and all was well. But, without warning, there was a loss of steering. Leonard was at the helm while Ian was down below, adjusting the computer we use for navigating in addition to our paper charts. Ian took the helm and Leonard went below to check what was going on. By now *Faoin Spéir* was beginning to toss about, flailing and floundering at the mercy of the sea. Ian tried to help her along by tweaking the ropes that hold the sails in place, with limited success. When Leonard established that we had lost helm and we needed to use the emergency tiller, he first went forward and took down the headsail and the mainsail, using a harness, and clipped on to the jackstays. Even the thought of this action makes me want to weep with fear. But it had to be done to stabilise the boat, otherwise she would have been at the mercy of the wind as well as the sea, and the danger to us would be have been so much greater.

So, Leonard fitted the emergency tiller with a struggle, and tried to turn us around for the port of Cork. We were approximately 15 miles out to sea. That journey was made out in less than three hours, but it took roughly seven hours to get back in. It was rough, we were bounced around, everybody felt sick, it was hard to focus and keep calm. We considered making a MAYDAY call and agreed we would wait five minutes, but by then the rudder was working and we started to make way, albeit slowly, in the right direction.

This time we were working against the tides and heading into the wind. It was horrendous and the vomiting started. There was, however, a good side for me, which was that Luke and Ella slept through all this and I was very happy that this was the case.

Leonard was now steering the boat using the tiller, sitting down below in the aft cabin, unable to see out, and Ian was directing him using hand signals because, with the engine running with the cover off, nothing could be heard. The pitching and rolling was immense and the vomiting continued. But we did not have the luxury of giving in to the sickness, we had to work to get back to harbour.

There was an almighty crash down below as one of the cupboards emptied its contents, and when this woke Ella, she emerged from her cabin, terrified, looking for reassurance. She received some but not as much as we would've liked to have given her. She tucked in beside me on the floor of the cockpit and she joined the group vomit. Vomit begets more vomiting. But gradually we were moving towards Cork, bit by bit.

As we got into the shelter of land, the swell reduced, as did the vomiting. The sun became warmer and we began to hope that all would be well for us. And still poor Leonard, feeling utterly miserable, steered us blindly. Occasionally he would stick his head up and steer with his foot to get a breath of air. Luke joined us in the cockpit, having completed his vomit in the toilet, and moaned about the fact that he should have risen sooner!

As we got closer to Crosshaven there was palpable relief for everybody. But we still had some work to do. Crosshaven on a sunny Saturday afternoon brings the world and her mother out to sail and it would appear we met them all in the narrow channel on the way in. Can you imagine driving your car and the steering wheel falls off, and somebody sits in beside you and gives you a long stick with which to steer, then blindfolds you and tells you they'll instruct you where to go? Now imagine doing that on the motorway on the last Sunday before Christmas and you may have some idea of the stress of the situation that Leonard and Ian faced in trying to get us safely into harbour. It was all hands on deck, eyes peeled and clear guidance to get through the channel and on to the pontoon.

By the time we came alongside, truly there was not a whole nerve intact between the five of us. When we tied up, the relief was enormous. We were all safe and *Faoin Spéir* was safe! It felt like we had all survived a long and drawn-out car crash.

As I got off the boat, I miscalculated the drop and slipped and fell. My feet ended up in the sea but luckily I had not let go of the stanchions. Ian and Leonard grabbed me, saving me from total immersion. However, my mobile phone slipped out of my pocket and now rests silently on the seabed. This was the proverbial straw breaking the camel's back. I think the terror, the physical hurt and the humiliation of the fall just broke me, and I dissolved into tears. Poor

Luke and Ella were getting distressed, so I left to get myself together. Ian took the kids for food and Leonard and I chatted for a while. I took some time alone and gathered myself together. We all did, in our own way.

We've had a scare, it has left us somewhat shaken and has raised some issues. We were disappointed not to be in the Scilly Isles en route to France. We have worked so hard for four years in the pursuit of this dream and now it feels like we are stuck. It also feels wrong to whine – we are all safe and well, and *Faoin Spéir* is in tip-top form. We managed a very tough situation and kept calm, finding the answer and working patiently despite our fear and sickness, and I am proud of us. A bit of me wants to give up and go home, a bit of me wants to continue on our journey, but mostly I am just tired and I want to sleep. We have since discovered that the cable in the helm snapped, probably fatigue after 42 years of extensive sailing. We are trying to replace it as I write. And then, we will get back on the horse and try again.

The aftermath

After we returned from the initial attempt at the Isles of Scilly, it took some searching for the replacement parts to make repairs. The steering cable that went from the base of the binnacle to the rudderstock had failed inside the pinion block. Repair may have been an option if I still had access to the workshop at school, but I figured if the cable had failed at that point, how much time remained for the rest of it? The difficulty was that the Morse cable, which was original to the boat, had not been in production since the early 1980s. Modern equivalents were not designed to deal with the same loads and most boats of our size now had hydraulic systems. As luck would have it, in my research online, I happened across a British company that claimed to 'make any Morse cable to order'. A couple of emails and a few phone calls later, and it turned out they could not in fact make 'any Morse cable to order'. Well, it was my own fault for allowing the internet to get my hopes up. It was looking increasingly likely that we'd have to replace the existing system with a hydraulic one.

In a last-ditch attempt to save our meagre bank balance, I redoubled my efforts online and found, in Hollywood, Florida, a near identical part, which had sat on a shelf for the past 30 years. There it lay, unopened, unused and forgotten, waiting to rescue the *Faoin Spéir* project. I say 'near identical' because it was actually 12 inches longer than needed, but I could live with that. Obviously some store was selling off all its old stock on eBay, and here it was – just what I was after, for US$200 plus shipping. This was far cheaper than the £1,800 it was going to cost for a hydraulic system. I made an offer of US$100, citing the shipping costs as the reason for my low ball. The seller duly accepted, and for the princely sum of £130, I had the cable needed to get us underway once more.

Once I had identified the day of departure, allowing for good weather, calm seas and a full moon, I made our passage plan. I emailed it to an experienced cruising friend and also had a chat with Wietse Buwalda, the marina owner, about it. Both agreed that my plan was sound. I half-heartedly sent a couple of texts and emails to a few sailing friends to see if they'd be interested in joining us, so as to take the pressure off the long watches, but none were available.

To a new country

The day of departure was disturbingly normal. We got up and had breakfast. We took a stroll to the local shop in Crosshaven for milk and bread and the like. The plan was to leave with the outgoing tide. I didn't want to leave too early because I didn't want to risk arriving before daybreak to a strange port, especially one as infamous as the Isles of Scilly. I recall stopping into Wietse to thank him for his help and advice, and being greeted with 'Are you not going to the Scillys?' The question sounded quite surreal. Yes, I was indeed going to the Scillys, but I didn't have any packing to do, I'd not got up at some ungodly hour that would normally signify the start of a grand adventure. Quite the opposite in fact; I'd gone about my morning as though I was going to embark on nothing more than reading a book in the afternoon. So I remarked that we would hop on the outgoing tide, as though we had a train to catch.

In truth, I was fearful and anxious but I dealt with it in the way I always do before going to sea: I recognise it, but also recognise that as the skipper I have to carry on regardless of my anxieties. I was, after all, the only sailor on board. I had the decisions to make and at that point, while it would have been easier to stay, I could see no better opportunity to go. Weather, wind, sun and moon were all in our favour, and it was important that the crew experience no further calamities for a while since our last outing.

The time finally arrived. With no one to wave us off and no fanfare, we slipped the lines at 1105 hours on 20 October 2016 and made the scheduled outgoing tide, which gave us a 2-knot push out of Cork Harbour and into a host of firsts.

Once clear of any navigational hazards, we had lunch and I popped below for a 30-minute nap at about 1600 hours before taking on the rest of the trip. We were, at this point, out of sight of land for the first time. We could stand and look in all directions, and see nothing but water. No features to guide us and no harbour to aim for. Many experienced sailors had advised us to go for a day sail over the horizon and back, six hours straight out and six hours back, just to see how the crew (myself included) felt about exposing a small boat to the open ocean. In our haste to ready the boat and tie things up on land, we never did get around to it. Looking at the position where the helm failed, I figure we must have been out of sight of land then, but there was so much else going on that we hadn't taken any notice.

So here we were, the four of us in our small boat, no land in sight and no one freaking out. Life is good. The trip continued in a fashion that might make more experienced sailors bored but for me, uneventful is just how I like it.

Later that night, I found myself alone at sea. All below were sleeping, or at the very least resting, and I sat in the cockpit, lights out and under a full moon. We went a full ten hours that night without sighting another vessel. Occasionally I would pop below to make a coffee, or grab a snack, leaving 'bungee' to helm. (I have found *Faoin Spéir* to be such a well-behaved boat that once balanced on the wind and sea, I can leave her for ten minutes at a time to keep her course. If I clip a bungee cord to the helm, then I've seen her keep her course for half an hour without adjustment.)

Morning came, and I was witness to a beautiful sunrise. There is something very special about a sunrise at sea. It's not so much the beauty of the image, although it is beautiful. For sailors everywhere, it's a timestamp, the marker that says 'It's another day, and before the sun goes down, we'll be in port.' Sailing, because it's so slow moving, means that covering any great distance will take a great deal of time. When sailors talk of crossing the Atlantic, they measure the distance in days rather than miles. Many are the times that I've heard 'two nights, three days' as the forecast for our intended crossing of the Bay of Biscay; never once has anyone said that it's 330 miles from Brest to La Coruna. Ticking off the miles in a long passage means little to a sailor when compared with ticking off the hours and days, and there is nothing that signifies that passing of a day like sunset and sunrise.

After coffee, I slipped into the harness and clipped on to the jackstay. We have a rule on board that regardless of the conditions, if we are out at sea, the harness goes on when leaving the cockpit. The purpose of my excursion was to raise our first courtesy flag. I'm not sure how it is for sailors from other nations, but sailing from Ireland, particularly from the west or south coasts, it's quite a distance to reach another country. For us it meant a 140 nautical mile trip in open water, and so raising that courtesy flag was like receiving a personal achievement award, and recognising the efforts of the four years' work that went into readying both boat and crew. Here we were, completely independent, a crew making their first offshore passage to another country. It's the 'independent' bit that really gives me that warm feeling of having achieved something. If there had been a more experienced sailor on board with us for that crossing, I'm not sure it would have felt quite so momentous.

Courtesy flag up, crew well rested and breakfast served, all we were short of now was our first sight of a foreign land. 'I see it! I see it!' 'Where? Where?' 'There it is again!' Such was the swell that only from the top of the waves could we see the low-lying islands off our bow. Now, for those of you who have gone before us, you'll appreciate what happens next. Nothing, nothing happens next. It's like driving to Disneyland and seeing a signpost for 'Disneyland, 250 miles'. After travelling for 24 hours and sighting your destination, it's still going to take at least another four hours before you arrive. But this is just another indicator that you are making progress towards your goal. Every boat is different, but it is useful to know your boat's typical 'duration to the horizon'. For us, we know that once we see a headland or island or whatnot, we are about four hours from that point.

Upon closing the four-hour gap, we lined up on our final approach to the harbour in Hugh Town, on St Mary's island, the largest of the Scilly Isles. My first official use of the radio was my call to the harbourmaster in Hugh Town. I told him who we were and restrained myself from saying something like, 'Yes, yes, we are the boat that just made that amazing voyage from the far-off land called Ireland.' Instead, I opted to tell them our length and draught, and asked if they could advise us on a suitable visitor's mooring. Even if you have done adequate research before arriving in a new port, it is wise to radio the harbourmaster for advice; he/she has the most up-to-date information and is happy to direct you to a suitable space.

Within ten minutes or so, we were approaching our selected buoy from an empty mooring field (it was October, after all). Picking up a mooring buoy was old hat at this stage – we must have done it at least three times by that point. Line on, engine off, hugs all around and even a tear or two.

Sailors around the world make passages like this every day. And this is the amazing thing about sailing;

such a passage, though commonplace, is never common for the people on board. Whether you are rounding a headland to a port just 30 miles away, or making a 21-day crossing of the Atlantic, the act of successfully moving your home, its contents and inhabitants, independent of any other entity, to a new destination is always something to be celebrated.

15

Life on board

I hesitate to use the word 'advice' when I talk about how we sail and what we might do in such and such a position. We simply do that which suits our sailing style as a family rather than any individual level or desire. This means that occasionally some might feel that we're not pushing hard enough while at other times the same person might feel we're pushing too hard. Essentially, the buck stops with the skipper, and one of the skipper's fundamental jobs is to find the right balance between the needs of the crew and the needs of the boat. The main aim is to get from A to B in good time, and with a happy and comfortable crew. So keep in mind that the vast majority of 'sailing advice' in this book comes from a place of comfort first. We tend to leave the adrenaline to others, preferring to move our home from place to place with the least possible fuss.

A good example of our approach relates to our tactics during storms, hurricanes and all sorts of other horrible weather beasties. What do we do in a storm? The answer is 'We don't'. What I mean by this is that we don't do storms. It may seem impossible, but one can sail the globe for an entire life and never experience more than a force 5. With today's weather prediction services and access to information, avoiding storms has become the norm for liveaboard cruisers. If, like most liveaboards, most of your passage-making is three days or less, the weather forecast is very accurate. Even when it comes to ocean crossing, you can greatly increase your likelihood of a pleasant passage by travelling at the optimal times and following the safest route.

It seems that every sailor has a story of being caught in horrendous weather conditions, and the next time you meet one ask them how it came about. I would wager that almost all of the stories start with 'Well, we had to get to such and such for Jimmy's flight', or 'We only had two weeks before we had to be in...', or 'I had work on Monday'. On board *Faoin Spéir*, we just don't have these kinds of deadlines. All our friends and relations know by now not to plan anything around us because we probably won't be where we think we'll be. Non-sailors in particular don't always get this, but when we explain that there are so many variables involved in moving a small boat about the ocean, and how if we commit to a deadline it may put us under pressure to sail when it's unsafe, they always rethink their plans. What works well for most of our visitors is to wait until we reach a particular country, and then to fly to us and hire a car or, in the case of continental Europe, bring their own car. This way, they can find us wherever we are.

So, our number one storm tactic? Throw the calendar away, sail when it suits, relax when it doesn't.

Crossing the English Channel

Every country with a coastline has its own version of the English Channel – a passage that serves as a gateway to the 'next level' in a sailor's story. Such a passage usually requires a skipper to plan for weather, heavy traffic, complex buoyage and strong currents. In the case of the Channel, it's got them all in abundance. The English Channel has the advantage of being only 20 miles wide around Dover, but it is the busiest shipping channel in the world. There are many, many resources that will tell you *how* to cross the Channel, so I won't go into it here other than to say that time is your friend. I must have said it a hundred times in different ways: the more time you have, the easier it will be to pick a day when it all comes together.

We made our Channel crossing from Ramsgate, Kent to Boulogne-sur-Mer, Pas-de-Calais, a 35-mile route. It was mid-June so we had long days, and the tides were such that a 10.30am departure would be just right. How civilised is that? To sail from one country to another after a lazy morning and an arrival that lines up nicely with dinner? The weather was set fair, force 2–3, and we had blue skies and a swell of less than a metre. We really had near-perfect conditions for a family crossing for the first time. I say 'near', because there was a haze that reduced visibility down to about a mile. The good thing about this was we saw only four ships in the entire crossing, and one of those was the Channel Lightship! But seriously, if you are truly a long-term liveaboard cruiser, take full advantage of your 'non-deadline' life. With patience, you will find exactly the conditions that suit you and your crew.

I learned a very useful lesson that day, one that has comforted me when setting out on many passages considered to be 'challenging': there are few sights more comforting than seeing several other boats slipping the lines at exactly the same time as you. It's a reassuring thing to know that a few other boats have independently arrived at the same plan as you, reassurance that repeated itself at the Alderney Race, Chenal du Four and the Raz de Seine; all names that previously gave me nightmares. I imagine I'd be quite worried if I set out and found we were the only boat making passage at the time.

Health and safety on board

M Maintaining health as a long-term cruiser is easier in some ways than it is on land. Your life is slower and so more manageable, and for the most part it is more relaxing. That is not to say that it is easier, because it is physically more strenuous. Even moving about the boat is a workout, as your balance is challenged and you use parts of you that you had forgotten all about. As on land, the simplest ways to maintain your health are as follows:

- get adequate sleep and rest
- eat a healthy, balanced diet
- exercise regularly
- drink lots of water
- protect your skin from the sun
- keep your alcohol consumption to recommended weekly limits
- do something you enjoy, every day
- enjoy some quiet time to yourself every day

This is as true for children as it is adults, but as any parents will know, you are responsible for your child's health too. There will be a period of adjustment when you move on board and your family will likely encounter the excitement of living in a new way and in unfamiliar climates. Take some time to adapt and make sure everyone drinks enough and covers up when in the sun.

Staying safe on your boat

There are people who would never consider a life at sea because they deem it unsafe and intimidating. In some way they are right; the sea is a powerful force and it deserves to be treated with respect. Keeping everyone safe on board requires serious thought and planning. The boat is home and as such is safe, but it has many potential hazards and these have to be managed. Even tied up in the marina, there are risks that need to be addressed. Marinas are full of cleats, lines, ropes, moving boat lifts, moving boats, and wet and sometimes narrow walkways, which can be even more slippery in wet or icy conditions. Falling into the water is a possibility and it is helpful to prepare children in particular for this eventuality without turning them into nervous wrecks.

- Get your child/ren swimming as early as possible.
- Insist on lifejackets or buoyancy aids if young children are out and about in the marina.
- Help your child to develop an awareness of hazards in the marina.
- Seek and find the emergency swim ladders in the marina.
- Teach children how to tread water.
- Teach children to stay still in the water in order to conserve energy, and to shout for help.
- Teach children to get help immediately if they see somebody struggling in the water or they witness somebody falling in.
- If the marina has no emergency swim ladders, identify boats with swim decks that can be used to get out of the water.

Use games and play to teach children water and marina safety. In this way, you reduce anxiety but raise awareness, which in turn gives children power and their own peace of mind.

Using the dinghy

As you can imagine, the transfer from your sailboat to a smaller boat can be dangerous. It is important to have a procedure in place and an emergency plan should somebody end up in the water. It goes without saying that each person must wear a lifejacket during the boat-to-boat transfer, especially when young children are involved.

For many long-term cruisers, the dinghy is the family 'runabout' and older children often use them to visit other cruisers or to explore a new area. In the same way as teaching your teenage son or daughter to drive a car, it takes time and effort to teach them how to operate the dinghy safely. First and foremost, they will need to know the dinghy's capacity, how to deal with falling out of it and what to do if it overturns. It is also advisable to carry the hand-held VHF radio on every excursion in the dinghy. Following simple rules keeps everyone safe and safety-conscious.

A safe home

For long-term cruisers, their boat is their home. As with any home, there are potential safety hazards. As we have already mentioned, there are many trip hazards in the marina. Once out of the marina, the boat is always in motion, even when moored or anchored, and this takes some getting used to. When the boat is underway at sea the movement is much stronger and more forceful, so even greater care has to be taken. Always exercise caution and awareness by adopting the following best practices.

- Ensure that handrails and other handholds are positioned at suitable heights for both adults and children.
- Wear shoes and sandals to avoid stubbing your toes.
- Ports and hatches need to opened and closed with care.
- Use bungee cords or nets to secure any items that can fall from shelves.
- Keep presses and lockers securely closed and open with caution, taking into account that what is inside has likely shifted since it was placed there.
- Keep the boat tidy and belongings stowed. Not only does this create space but it also reduces the risk of tripping and ensures less mess to tidy if the boat moves unexpectedly.
- Use nets or lee cloths to keep little ones safe while playing or napping.
- Keep long hair tied up to prevent it getting caught in winches and ropes.

Preparing for passage

When the boat is underway it is a majestic sight. However, it can create a lot of movement. Anything loose above and below deck will sashay at best or at worst turn into projectiles when making passage. Everything has to be secured and stowed, and a procedure put in place for this, or your boat could be wrecked and your crew injured. The important thing to remember is even the most benign object can be lethal if it is flying around a boat. Some of the following suggestions may be useful, but it is important to say that each crew has its own routine around preparing for passage.

When sailing you are acutely aware of the sounds of the boat, so stowing should also take account of reducing unnecessary banging sounds by securing all locks. On *Faoin Spéir*, we manage this by placing cushions and spare towels in the presses in the galley in order to fill up empty spaces. Secure all presses and storage areas, and avoid opening them during passages.

Keep to hand anything the crew needs while at sea, such as toys, pyjamas, toothbrushes, a warm jumper, a book, a torch, a drink and sunscreen. It is useful for each crew member to keep these items in a small, soft bag that is readily accessible but stowed securely. Any food, drinks, cooking utensils, crockery and cutlery to be used during the passage should be stored safely, tightly and in an accessible space for ease of preparation and serving. We have plastic mugs with lids that can be used for serving everything from porridge to stew while safely avoiding spills and keeping food hot. Always have a small first aid kit to hand (see page 149). Leave enough time for preparation, as speed is the enemy of safety. On *Faoin Spéir* we usually secure the boat the night before for an early passage.

Faoin Spéir's below-deck departure checklist

- Stow everything that can move by packing items as tightly as possible.
- Cover all bottles and jars with old socks to prevent noise and breakage.
- Fill any empty spaces in galley presses with cushions or towels.
- Rearrange loose cans in the food press.
- Use silicone grip mats to secure items on the table and worktop, such as maps.
- Set up the computer for navigation and secure with a bungee.
- Secure the oven door with a bungee.
- Secure the rubbish bin with a bungee.
- Double-check the cabins and secure anything loose.
- Check all ports and hatches are closed securely.
- Check the latch is secured on the rear cabin.
- Secure the galley press doors.
- Secure the pantry doors.

- Cover the cooker.
- Stow the kettle and coffee pot safely in the sink with a tea towel.
- Turn on the AIS transponder and VHF radio, and complete a radio check.

Safe space

When travelling with young children and prior to commencing the passage, determine a safe space for them to hang out in while at sea. Their bunk is usually a good area for this. If things get a bit rough they can raise the lee cloth, or an adult can help them to do so, and they can use this space to play, read or draw and feel safe, preferably with their siblings or a parent where possible.

Emergencies

Nobody wants to be involved in an emergency but they are a fact of life and as such it is essential to prepare for them. Cruising requires this preparation, too. The key to good preparation is taking into consideration all possibilities and determining a plan for each. Regular reviews of safety equipment, such as fire extinguishers, smoke alarms, flares, bilge alarms, ropes and jackstays, keep everyone safe. All crew members should know where the sea cocks are, how to start the engine and how to use the VHF radio to make a PAN PAN and MAYDAY call. It is essential that the crew practises the man-overboard manoeuvre – the hope, of course, is that you never have to use it but nevertheless it is crucial to be familiar with the procedure. Everyone should know where the liferaft is and the grab bag, and be drilled in the procedure for launching the liferaft. Most importantly, discussing emergencies in a matter-of-fact manner without raising anxiety is crucial.

Time for change

One of the things I love most, but also find challenging, about the cruising lifestyle is flexibility. Most people consider flexibility a good thing and of course it can be. For the cruiser, flexibility takes many forms. It can mean preparing the boat and crew for departure and then getting a funny feeling about the conditions and deciding to stay put, maybe for another month! It can mean leaving your cruising life and returning to land for a few months. It can mean changing your destination at the drop of a hat for completely subjective reasons. Whichever way you look at it, flexibility is mostly a good thing. However, occasionally it can lead to unpredictability and feeling stuck.

When we left Ireland, we planned to head to the Rio Guadiana on the Portugal–Spain southern border for the winter. However, this trip never materialised, for a number of reasons. Instead, we spent six months living just outside London. This proved to be very productive for us, although Luke expressed impatience to get to Spain on occasion, as he was anxious to play soccer there. In cases such as his, we have to remind the children that we have all the time in the world. I guess that is the point; there is room for flexibility because we are not constrained by time *at all*. Whether you regard that as a positive, a negative or simply a fact of life, the important thing is to check in with your crew members to make sure that everyone's needs are being met when changing plans at a moment's notice.

When I encounter people now and they ask me where I live, my standard reply is 'I live on a boat'. Although they are asking for a location, I usually reply by describing my accommodation. I think this more than any other question highlights the change involved in becoming cruisers and living this dream. Our accommodation is a boat and this allows us to travel wherever the wind blows. People have all kinds of ideas about you when you say you live on a boat. The most common assumptions are that you live on a fancy yacht and are on a permanent holiday or living a fantasy lifestyle of partying and boozing. Those assumptions constitute living the dream, the Deluxe Version! We *are* living the dream, but we are living *our* dream. Of course, cruising can be all those things but for the vast majority of us it is about a simpler lifestyle, being able to spend more time with those we love and having time to breathe, think and smell the roses (is there a sea equivalent for smelling the roses?). For me, living the dream is primarily about having time to connect with the people we encounter on our travels and to be enriched by the experience of travelling.

Birthdays

When Luke and Ella celebrated their first birthday as liveaboard cruisers, they were 14 years old and they wanted a birthday celebration. I must confess, I was feeling anxious about the whole affair. Christmas and birthdays are unforgettable and really you want them to be unforgettable for the right reason. At that point we were spending time in Port Launay, France, so Leonard and I decided to host a birthday barbecue. We don't own a barbecue, so off we went to purchase one. We hosted the event on the village green, where we were joined by locals, fellow travellers, invited guests and casual party attendees. It turned out to be a joyful, fun celebration, filled with family and new friends.

Living the dream is all about adventure and change, but we get most of our joy from the people we meet along the way. I could never have anticipated that new friends would become such a part of the fabric of our liveaboard lives. I know visiting new places is important, too, but we have berthed, anchored or moored for a night and left as quickly as we could because we felt unsafe or unwelcome. In truth, those experiences are rare but they are useful in developing your instincts and learning to follow your gut. But what makes a place, in my estimation, is the relationships and friendships you develop with the people you meet along the way. For me, people are how you really experience a place and get to know it.

Slowing down

L I have always considered myself to be a person who operates at an easy pace. Not that I work slowly, I just simply don't 'do' frantic. Frantic isn't efficient and I love efficiency. On more than one occasion, work colleagues have commented on how 'nothing fazes' me, or how I always seem quite relaxed. I honestly thought I was, until I moved on to the boat. It took a full year of being a liveaboard for me to really understand and accept the idea of 'slowing down'. Again, this doesn't necessarily mean working slowly, but it does mean working and living at the natural pace and rhythm of the life you've chosen.

Let me give you an everyday example. Suppose you decide you fancy a cup of tea but you discover you're out of milk. My typical response on land would be to pop down to the local shop in the car and pick up some milk, a chore that would have taken 10 minutes, max. On the boat, however, we have no car, we may be anchored off and even if we are tied up in a town quay, it's usually 30 minutes to the nearest shop. In our experience, getting that milk would take about an hour and a half on average. I recall one scorching hot day (scorching for those of us used to the higher latitudes). I kayaked 2 miles, then walked a further 4½ miles to buy some oranges, milk and treats for the crew, before making the same return journey, covering 13 miles in total. And this was during the summer in Kent!

We have all had those family holidays where we arrive at our destination for a week or two, leaving our woes behind, enjoying a lie-in in the mornings and generally slowing down. But if we really look objectively at holidays, they are often just as structured as the working week. There are sights to see, a set time for breakfast in the hotel, the tour bus leaves bang on 8am. In many ways, people 'need a holiday after their holiday'!

For months after moving aboard, I found myself in this place, particularly when it came to passage planning, weather forecasting and all things related to moving the boat and crew safely from A to B. We had reached the Rade de Brest, a bay in Brittany, and for weeks I had been plotting and replotting the impending Biscay crossing. Mary, Luke and Ella were not wholly confident about taking independent watches, and so the majority of the sailing would fall to me. At this stage, we had covered more than 2,500 miles at sea, without using any form of autohelm. But our longest passage was only 35 hours up to that point, and *Faoin Spéir* is a kindly boat that balances well, with little input in most conditions. My projection of four days for the crossing was on a different level. It would require a structured watch system, so that I may get some regular sleep in order to focus on a safe and successful passage. For weeks I looked at all sorts of solutions. Perhaps I could phone around some sailing friends to come and crew, or set up the electronic autohelm and run the engine while I slept, or even port hop around the bay... Then it dawned on me: what was the hurry? We were in this for the long run, we had no plan to return, so whom were we racing? Relax and breathe. And with that realisation, that's exactly what we did.

In the end, we decided that our ideal crossing of Biscay would be to sail it without outside help. The best way to achieve this in both comfort and safety was to spend the winter and spring in Brittany, where we would work on our sailing skills and get the whole crew to a place where each could stand watch independently. I struggled for a while with this decision, thinking that we would be a year behind. But a year behind what?

As it turned out, we ended up having some wonderful experiences that we would have otherwise missed out on. We wintered in a little village on the River Aulne at the head of the Rade du Brest. The Nantes–Brest canal begins about 10½ miles upriver, and just beyond the first lock is Port Launay. We hadn't heard of the village until one day Mary and I were strolling about the town of Camaret-sur-Mer on the Crozon peninsula. We found ourselves in a second-hand bookstore, and in a box in one part of the store we found some sailing books, one of which was an English copy of the North Biscay sailing pilot from 2005, at a princely sum of £3. So we added yet another book to our already bulging library. In the first few pages there was mention of Port Launay, and how no cruising sailboat should leave Brittany without paying a visit. Decision made, we headed into the Rade du Brest, and after sitting out a force 8 at anchor, made our way up the Aulne for a two-day visit to Port Launay and a supply run to Châteaulin. It was twelve months later that we made our way back down the river. How is that for slowing down?

Our decision to slow down allowed us to develop friendships that will last a lifetime, our French improved immensely, ticking the home-schooling box, and we were comfortably off the sea for what turned out to be a very harsh winter. Mary's mother was ill and sadly passed away during this period, and I imagine if we had not slowed down, managing all that comes with dealing with the loss of a family member would have been so much more difficult. In addition, accepting that we were neither behind nor ahead, we were simply living and cruising at our pace, came to me like nirvana. Almost overnight, everything became easier and more enjoyable.

Clearing in and out of new countries

I am always a little apprehensive when clearing into a new country. Even within the European Union, where one can drive unimpeded across borders, there can be a lot of red tape to negotiate. It seems that there are different requirements to be met in each country, or in some cases in different regions of the same country. However, almost all require use of the 'Big Four':

- passports
- registration

- certification of competence (ICC or IPC)
- certificate of insurance

These essential documents need to be kept in a safe and accessible place. We keep several photocopies of each in a folder, which will make it easier to request replacements should the originals ever be lost or stolen (something we have not had to deal with so far). Whenever the authorities need to make copies, they are often glad to accept one of ours, as it saves them a little extra work. We do carry a printer/scanner combo on board if more copies are needed, and we also keep digital scans of all of our important paperwork. This is useful as the ultimate backup or for sending documents via email.

Beyond the Big Four, it may be necessary to carry regional permits for navigation, anchoring or scuba-diving, as is the case in Galicia, Spain. Off the coast of Galicia, there are several protected islands that are part of a marine national park, and while the permits are free and easy to obtain, you do need to apply for them in advance and make them available for presentation to the coastguard on request. This sort of information can be found in any good pilot book of the region in which you intend to sail.

Along with satisfying immigration, you may also encounter officials from customs and revenue. An encounter with these departments usually involves some simple form filling in order for you to declare you are not carrying contraband and your boat is VAT compliant. For

EU citizens, it only pops up when entering or leaving the EU Common Market.

In general, when dealing with officialdom it is vital to your peace of mind (and freedom) that you engage the official with patience, respect and a smile. Try to anticipate the documents they may need and have them with you. Remember, you're a guest, and behaving otherwise, or giving the official a hard time, is only going to impact on one person's needs – yours. One last thing: it doesn't hurt to try to use the local language.

16

Self-sufficiency

Sailing is a bit of an anomaly. It is an ancient skill and has remained pretty much the same for thousands of years. However, in the past 40 years, technology has improved to the point that there is an abundance of gadgets and accoutrements that make a sailor's life more comfortable and pleasant. Nonetheless, cruising does allow you the opportunity to live an alternative lifestyle, a simpler life altogether. I know there are many people who would consider living on a luxury yacht anything but 'simple', but most liveaboard cruisers with families don't live on luxury yachts. They live on medium-priced boats that are safe, sturdy and often able to take the punishment of a family. As a result, the boat requires near-constant maintenance and general upkeep.

Most liveaboard cruisers take care of their own boats and undertake any work that needs doing themselves. Leonard always says that there are those who can afford boats (and we all know what that means) and then there are those who can fix them. We definitely belong to the second category. But may I respectfully suggest that most liveaboard cruisers belong to that category. The lifestyle by its very nature does encourage self-sufficiency, problem-solving and competence. It occurs to me that this may be what people mean when they say to us, 'I could never do what you are doing.' I had always thought it was the bobbing about on the sea on a boat that put them off, but perhaps it is the self-sufficiency, problem-solving and learning a whole new set of skills.

Self-sufficiency is an interesting concept in the modern age of globalisation. When I was a child the British sitcom *The Good Life* aired on TV. *The Good Life* was the story of a young couple living in English suburbia who gave up the rat race and their nine-to-five jobs to live an alternative lifestyle and become self-sufficient in their small, modern house and back garden, much to the dismay of their upwardly mobile neighbours. As you can imagine, in the tradition of great British comedy, this clash of personalities leads to great hilarity. But the 'alternative' couple always maintains a can-do attitude and when their hard work failed, that attitude became 'make do'. I think this more than anything else embodies the concept of self-sufficiency. It is the fundamental belief that you can survive with what is available, or simply make do. In becoming self-sufficient, you take responsibility for providing for yourself and your family rather than handing over all your power as a consumer to a global organisation that is telling you what you need and want. Being self-sufficient means that you are careful about what you consume and only do so on a 'needs must' basis, while having due regard for the impact of your consumption on the environment and other people.

This is an ideal that we, and many other cruisers, aspire to every day. Sometimes we fail and this is a learning curve for all of us, but for us personally, becoming self-sufficient is as important as getting safely from A to B. It means trying to reduce our consumption of power and water, using the power we generate from the sun to maximum impact and doing without it when we do not have it. We use water sparingly, both on the boat and when we have access to it on land. We use our gas cooker to its maximum potential when cooking. We use environmentally friendly products, such as soaps, detergents and shampoos. We buy recyclable items and avoid single-use plastics. We make use of recycling facilities to dispose of our cans, tins and bottles. We walk as much as possible and use public transport, which is easy when you don't have a car!

I should clarify that we are not in the least bit sanctimonious about our lifestyle. Cruising requires that we travel as lightly as possible and live on a tight budget. Therefore, it is easy for us to be self-sufficient and live a simple, consumer-lite lifestyle. Luke and Ella do not attend school and so are not subject to the relentless influence of consumerism that is particularly rampant among their age group. We also have very different consumer needs as cruisers. I do, however, know that being more self-sufficient than we were in our land life gives us tremendous freedom and the power to live the kind of life we want to live. Sometimes that means we have to make do. However, making do is a small price to pay.

The 'can do' attitude is, in my opinion, an essential part of cruising. You will almost certainly need to gain the competence to live life almost off-grid. Clearly, being able to sail and manage the boat is one of the skills you'll need to master. Manoeuvring the boat using the variables of wind and tide under sail and keeping everyone on board safe also takes training, practice and experience. I think the measure of a good sailor is maintaining clear judgement in all conditions and states of wakefulness/sleep deprivation. It is also knowing your limits and using your crew to maximum effect. There is a wonderful feeling of freedom and achievement in arriving in a new country under sail, knowing that you are there by your own power and skill. There is no right or wrong way to do it, and each crew does it in its own way according to its members' competence.

Engines

Sailboats have engines, and engines plus salt water equals a lot of maintenance. It's a fact of life. Most liveaboard cruisers travel with spare engine parts and can repair their engine while at sea, and it appears to me that no matter how much you maintain the boat engine in port, if it is to break down, it will invariably do so at sea! This isn't a problem if you can hoist the sails and get on with repairs, but if that were the case, the sails would be up in the first place and there'd be no need for the engine. We've had several engine failures at times when we really needed our engine to work. The list is extensive: transmission failure as we were heading into berth with a 17-knot wind on our nose; a water coolant hose replacement while motoring in the choppy waters of the Île de Batz with rocky outcrops all around; impeller failure while sailing down the Channel to Le Havre with no wind... It is neither possible nor practical to call the mechanic in such situations; the engine needs to be fixed on the move, while you also ensure that the boat and crew are safe.

Ⓛ *Faoin Spéir* still has her original 35hp Chrysler Nissan four-cylinder diesel engine. If anything about that previous statement confuses you, my advice to you is that you conduct a little study into the mechanics of your auxiliary propulsion system. It may well be the case that you sail without a throbbing, smoky beast stinking up your sea air, but it is an unavoidable fact that the vast majority of sailboats now have an engine of some sort. An awkward side effect of this is that modern ports and marinas are designed with nimble, thruster-clad, big-engined boats in mind, and ageing ocean voyagers like *Faoin Spéir* can be quite the handful if you have a bit of a blow or current to contend with.

Although I love nothing more than setting out or berthing under sail, I recognise and enjoy the convenience of a healthy engine on board. With this in mind, if you go to sea expecting to use the engine, at least one person on board should know the absolute basics (see box overleaf).

Engine basics checklist

I can:

- access the engine bay (it's not always that straightforward)
- top up, check and identify appropriate oil and coolant levels in both the engine and gearbox
- change each of the fuel filters (most boats have more than one)
- check and clear the raw water filter
- recognise normal raw water out, what it looks like and sounds like
- replace an impeller and pulley belts (alternator, water pump)
- recognise overheating, as it's no good being able to replace a water pump impeller if you don't even know the engine is about to seize
- dip the fuel tanks in case of a faulty fuel gauge
- replace any one of the myriad hoses

The need for these skills crops up from time to time, and often while at sea. If you're lucky, it'll be while you have plenty of sea room, but you can't plan your breakdowns. You've been warned; don't let the learning go until you need the skill. Once the ship's designated engineer can tick all the boxes above, you can use it as a training list for everyone else on board.

The vast majority of sail training centres offer introductory courses on basic diesel engine understanding and maintenance. The RYA offers a one-day course that covers the following:

- the principles of diesel engine operation
- the systems and parts of the engine
- fault finding
- rectifying common problems
- bleeding the fuel system
- changing the impeller
- routine maintenance
- winter lay-up procedures

The important thing to remember if completing such a course is to practise your new-found skills regularly.

Another option is to look into evening classes in your area. Many towns run courses on motor maintenance and although the focus is often on cars, the engine, at its core, is the same. These courses (I used to teach them) would typically go through most, but not all of the RYA topics. Missing from the syllabus would be the changing of an impeller and winter lay-up procedures. You do, however, get the benefit of regular classes over a period of around eight weeks, thus more hands-on practice and reinforced learning.

Once you have some basic tuition under your belt, be it from a professional course or a friendly neighbour who enjoys tinkering with old cars, you can watch tutorials online or invest in a book on the subject, such as *The Adlard Coles Book of Diesel Engines*, by Tim Bartlett

(2011). However you progress, it is vital that you practise regularly.

Key skills

Ⓜ Many other systems on the boat need constant care. Similar to life on land, in which you unblock drains, change light bulbs, free up the toilet, mow the lawn, paint the fence, and replace the guttering, most of these tasks apply to boat life too. Ongoing maintenance jobs that require your attention on board include: cleaning; clearing; replacing parts; checking seals and sea cocks; emptying the bilge and cleaning it; washing down the decks; checking below the waterline for growth; painting and antifouling; checking lines, sheets and cleats; and making sure your batteries are fully charged. They are basic skills but are essential to the safe care and maintenance of all boat systems.

In addition to being a janitor you'll need to develop additional skills for the cruising life, including budgeting, cooking and baking, problem-solving, weather forecasting and knot tying. All of these make things as a cruiser so much easier and contribute to a self-sufficient and independent existence.

Budgeting

Budgeting is a skill in short supply, or at least in shorter supply than one would imagine. In some ways this is understandable, especially with the rise of the credit culture. In the present economic reality there is a tendency to borrow money through fixed-term loans or by maxing out credit cards to fund a particular lifestyle. However, this can often mean that people are not living within their means, or they do not know how to budget.

Budgeting is an essential life skill and one that is vital for cruising. You will need to learn how to assess what you consider an essential and what you consider a luxury. It may surprise you to learn what is really essential for you. It's a small price to pay for the freedom of living within your means.

Cooking and baking

I would say that cooking and baking are essential cruising skills to develop, but I know many cruisers who manage to live on frozen and/or tinned foods and avoid cooking altogether. I am of the opinion that the path you must follow is the one that suits your circumstances.

By cooking, I mean combining fresh ingredients to prepare a meal that will nourish you or your family. One cannot presume that this is a skill people possess. Today, convenience food, ready-cooked meals and takeaways have become the norm, and often with both partners in a relationship working outside the home, time is of the essence. In many ways, cooking becomes time-consuming and superfluous.

One of the joys of cruising is that it allows you to reclaim this time. Cooking, preparing, serving and enjoying food with your family becomes one of the supreme delights of a life on board. Baking also falls into this category — especially baking bread, though baking treats is useful too, especially if confined to the boat on a wet day with kids. In addition to affording you the freedom to stay on board rather than make the journey to the nearest shop or supermarket, fresh, home-baked bread is a great pleasure when at sea or at anchor. We have also been anchored or berthed in places — on islands, for example — where fresh bread is not a given and being able to make it for ourselves and others has been a huge comfort. It has also allowed us to make friends, begin conversations and swap our wares for fish and many other lovely things. Fortunately for us, bread is multicultural and as such it is an international currency, so never underestimate the benefits of learning how to bake.

Problem-solving

Problem-solving is a key life skill, no matter where you choose to live. Cruising, like all other aspects of life, presents its fair share of problems and all provide an opportunity to learn something new and move forwards.

We have faced all kinds of problems in our time cruising. One thing we've had to deal with is being down to our last £20, or at least needing to survive on it for longer than foreseen because we haven't been paid moneys owed. I get very panicky when we are low on cash, as it leaves us so vulnerable. So how do we manage in that situation? As with most problems, we sit down and we assess the situation. We take stock of what we have – a well-stocked larder, water and electricity, and very few outgoings. So what can we do to reduce costs for the period? We can avoid buying anything and use just what we have on board. If we feel we need to make money, we can get part-time jobs or look for gigs or do a little busking. We can also contact those who owe us money, to remind them of their tardiness and request a new payment date. We then follow all parts of the plan as agreed. I find it immensely helpful when dealing with any kind of problem to sit down with Leonard, assess the situation, seek reasonable workable solutions and then implement them.

Another, far more complex problem that faces many people, as well as cruisers, is how to manage the care of an elderly parent. How do you resolve your desire to live the life you want while providing for an elderly parent/s? My mother had dementia and the winter before she died, my brother and sisters were taking a day each to provide care. I wanted to play my part in the family and be at home to help take care of her too. So, Leonard and I agreed that I would fly home every five weeks and spend the week in Ireland looking after mother, giving everyone else in the family time off and me the chance to spend time with my ailing parent. However, when it became clear that she was deteriorating quickly, we all returned to Ireland for the winter, and this allowed me to do a day like everyone else and be at home for the end stages of my mother's life. I was grateful for our ability to problem-solve and having the flexibility that allowed us to move beyond our plans to find a solution that worked for everyone.

Weather forecasting

Ⓛ There's a saying that you know you live on a boat when you talk with your neighbours about the weather, and mean it. If it is your intention to live on a boat, even if you never intend moving said boat, you need to get to grips with the weather. I've mentioned elsewhere that our number one storm tactic is 'to not go'. Fortunately, modern weather forecasting is highly accurate for 24 hours, very accurate for three days and, well, you can probably make a plan for up to five days.

The difference between how we see the weather in our land lives and our boat lives is in the detail. On land, tomorrow might be described as windy, with some rain in the morning but brightening up in the afternoon. The same forecast when sailing would be chock-full of details on an hourly basis, such as wind direction and strength, exactly when and for how long rain might be falling, and at what time the sun will set or the moon rise. The influence of the wind is blatantly obvious to sailors making passage, but more than a few of us have ended up in a rolly anchorage or even an uncomfortable marina berth after a forecasted post-passage shift in wind direction went unnoticed. Whether at sea, or not, if you're on a boat, you need to understand the impact of weather and tides.

It can, however, take a lifetime of practice to learn how to read the weather based on the conditions and cloud formations. At sea, a rain shower, fog bank or a heavy gust all have obvious signs in the short term and you can often see them coming. Frank Singleton's *Reeds Weather Handbook for Sail and Power* (2014) is a great book to have to hand when it comes to looking to the sky for your forecast, and we do carry a copy on board. However, because most of our sailing consists of shorter passages (three days or less), we rely on the weather forecasting services that we receive through VHF radio or the internet.

Online weather services are quite excellent, and carry every conceivable piece of data a sailor could need. We usually use www.windy.com and www.passageweather.com. Windy, in particular, has an excellent animation function that allows you to see the movement of weather systems around the world. This is especially useful for longer ocean passages. A good example is crossing the Bay of Biscay. It's not enough to look at the local weather conditions for such a passage – the weather coming out of the Gulf of Mexico at the other side of the Atlantic will have a profound impact on the weather in Biscay next week. Through these websites, we can assess the big picture and begin to understand the interconnectedness of weather systems around the globe.

A useful exercise, and some entertainment for the crew while at anchor, is to engage in a little competitive weather forecasting. Select a specific time and day and have each member aboard predict the wind speed, or if rain is on the cards, at what time the first drops will land on the deck (taping a blue square of blotting paper to the deck saves any arguments!). It can be great fun, and you'd be amazed at how quickly everyone's forecasting skills develop, even the skipper's!

Knot tying

Sailors have long been known for their knot-tying skills and although I knew I should practise my knots while searching for and restoring *Faoin Spéir*, I never fully appreciated just how handy a skill knot tying is. There are many books available on a whole host of knots, *The Adlard Coles Book of Knots* by Peter Owen (2006) is an excellent source and with over 50 knots, I'm sure it will keep you going for some time.

For those of you who like your tuition in app form, there are many knot-tying tutorial apps to choose from, although I am reluctant to recommend any as they seem to come and go with increasing regularity. We have put instructional videos of a few of our favourites on our website, www.FaoinSpeir.com, along with an explanation as to where and how we use them on board. Here I'm going to focus only on the knots that we use most often, if not daily but certainly weekly, on *Faoin Spéir*. Before I continue, in the interest of quieting the pedants, of which I am often one, I'm going to refer to all of the following as 'knots' rather than heading down a rabbit hole filled with hitches, bends and shanks...

288

Bowline

If you don't know how to make a bowline, then learn it now... Go on, get a piece of rope or cord or your shoelace. The bowline is certainly the most commonly used knot on *Faoin Spéir*, and any other boat that I have frequented. Whether making fast a mooring line to a deck cleat, or a sail to a halyard, or lifting the dinghy on to the deck, the bowline is king. It doesn't slip, jam or come loose, and yet it is not difficult to untie with cold, wet hands. It's a quick and easy knot for creating a loop at the end of a rope, particularly useful when approaching a berth where a loop over a bollard or cleat can quickly reattach the boat to land. Once you are comfortable with the knot, practise tying it with one hand.

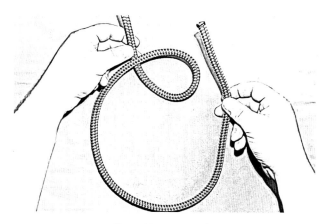

Bowline step 1.

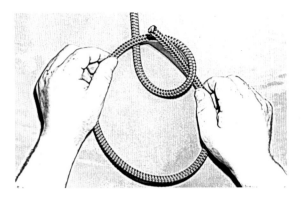

Bowline step 2.

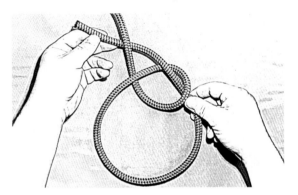

Bowline step 3.

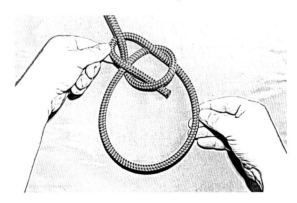

Bowline step 4.

Bowline step 5.

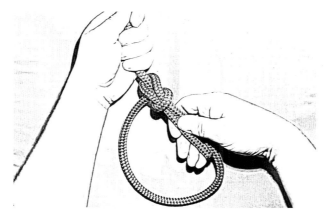

Bowline step 6.

Clove hitch

We use this knot with daily regularity in three places on board, and all three are typically related to the transition from sailing to resting. It's probably why I have a particular fondness for this simple and elegant knot. We use it for stowing hanked ropes on the pushpit rails, for hanging fenders from the stanchions and for tying the halyards off and away from the mast in order to prevent that insufferable frapping to which some sailors seem immune (usually the culprits). When we are tying these knots, it usually means we have at least a couple of days off. For added security, I'd often put in an extra turn, or half hitch, but you can play with it in your own time.

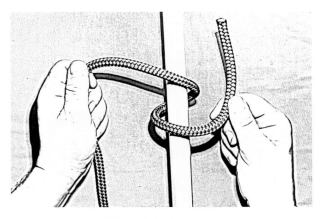

Clove hitch step 1.

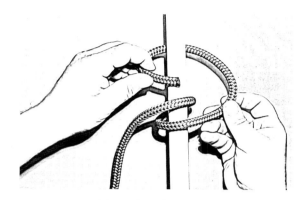

Clove hitch step 2.

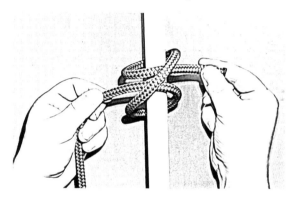

Clove hitch step 3.

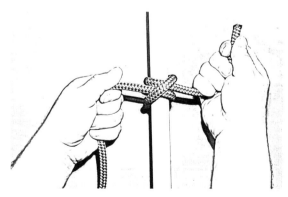

Clove hitch step 4.

Reef knot

Who'd have thought that a reef knot was for reefing sails? Certainly before engaging in my present lifestyle, I had never made the connection. As we tend to keep things simple on *Faoin Spéir*, we still reef the sails the old-fashioned way, tying off the reefing points to the boom while wishing we had in-mast furling and cursing the beam swell. Other than reefing and stowing (we don't have lazyjacks) the mainsail, we tend not to use the knot as much as the clove hitch and bowline, but where we do use it, it's the only knot for the job.

Knowing these three knots will take you a long way but don't let it stop there. Other knots that see regular use on board are:

- the figure-of-eight, as an ideal stopper or super secure loop
- the sheet bend, for joining ropes and ribbons
- the Prusik hitch or knot, which I tend to use for hanging clothes lines and hammocks from the forestay

There are also several ornamental knots that we try just for the fun of it. The important thing is to always have some rope to hand and to practise. It's just like learning a musical instrument – practice makes perfect.

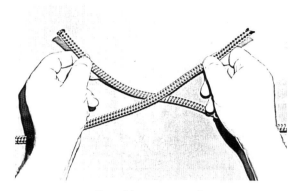

Reef knot step 1.

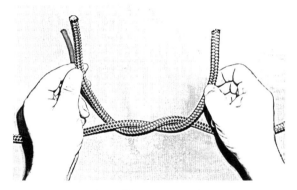

Reef knot step 2.

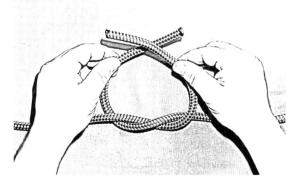

Reef knot step 3.

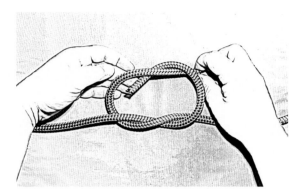

Reef knot step 4.

Reef knot step 5.

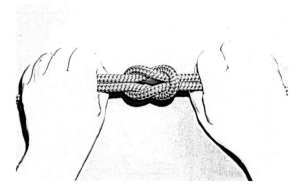

Reef knot step 6.

17

A woman's perspective

Ⓜ Among sailing and cruising heterosexual couples, there is a tendency for the boat to be skippered by the man. I'm not trying to generate a debate on gender equality in cruising couples, but for now this is how it is. Because of this, the ultimate decisions around tooling, equipping, planning and a host of other 'skipper' areas are filtered through a male perspective. Women can and do have an equal say in most of these decisions, but it's not always easy for one gender to identify or understand the needs of the other on board. So, here we will explore some liveaboard cruising issues from the female perspective. Gentlemen should read on too, as you may learn something new.

Identity

Slowing down was one of the most terrifying parts of moving on to the boat for me and it proved to be a real struggle. There was so much *time*, and then more time, and then even more time. The days were endless and I was disorientated and often felt useless. I think like most women, in my old life on land, the second I rolled out of the bed in the morning I hit the ground running. I had the table set for breakfast, kettle boiled, dishwasher emptied and first load of laundry in before I had even opened my eyes. I know from my own experience and that of other women who work both inside and outside of the home that our lives are filled with chores and busyness and constant production. In fact, I have heard female colleagues refer to the workplace as a respite from home, even though they were exceptionally productive in the workplace, too. I used to puzzle about that, but now I know the productivity of the workplace and the demands placed upon women in their homes are radically different. Unlike our children, our colleagues will respect both our personal space and our right to say no. Also, they tend not to encroach on us as we use the bathroom!

It is amazing just how much of our identity is tied up in what we *do*. It defines our life for the most part, how we organise our time, how much money we have, with whom we spend most of our day, our mental health and well-being, how people think of us and how we think of ourselves. It is how society labels us and we are expected to act in a certain way as a result. If you don't believe me, consider the mental picture you get when you hear any of the following: 'She's a stay-at-home mum', 'She's a nun', 'She's a journalist', 'She's a start-up CEO', not only do you have a mental image of what they look like but you also have an opinion about each. The truth is, if you lined up those four women and dressed them in black leggings and a black T-shirt with no make-up, what you have is simply four women.

I have worked since I was very young. As a young teenager I earned money as a babysitter and went into paid employment at the age of 15. I had never been unemployed, and any time I spent out of work was due to studying, illness, pregnancy or holidays. In addition to paid employment, I have volunteered my time to a variety of charities and community projects.

Part of moving on to the boat for me meant giving up the traditional nine-to-five role I had enjoyed and endured for most of my life. I found myself in a place of being unemployed for the first time, being incompetent when it came to sailing and knowing very little about how the boat worked, and it left me in a very vulnerable place. During that first year, I really struggled to slow down. I hated it, to be honest. I was not a teacher or a counsellor or a member of the drama group, I received very few texts or emails and I heard from very few people at all. I had disappeared and become a nonentity. I really struggled with two aspects of this: what I felt about myself and not really knowing who I was at all, and sometimes not recognising myself. In addition, I missed hearing from people, feeling like I was important to them or that I had something important to contribute. There was a vacuum in my life and I had no idea how to be. I was irritable and angry, and Leonard and the kids were tiptoeing around me. They were literally afraid to poke the bear.

It aggravated me even further to see that Leonard was taking to 'slowing down' like the proverbial duck to water. I know this might be the place to rant about how men and women have a different approach to productivity – and they do – but he was finding his own way and was competently beginning a new life without me. To be fair to him, Leonard did try to help me but I was raging and making life very difficult.

There was another issue. This was the life I wanted. I had worked for this and prepared for a life with more time and less stress, so what the heck was wrong with me?

What was wrong with me was that I was grieving. I think for me what I experienced in those first few months was not just losing work and my identity, but I also felt disconnected from my old life and like I did not belong anywhere. I was bereft. Now, this may seem dramatic and over the top, but on 1 November I wrote in my journal: 'I am miserable right now, I feel like nothing I have learnt my whole life is of any use at all.' Those were hard days, and I think slowing down and having the time to feel all of these emotions just made everything seem worse. However, those emotions also allowed me to experience the grief and work through it. Sometimes the only way through grief is through the grief.

You're not alone

It did seem odd to me, though, to be in this place emotionally when the new life was very much of my own choosing. I thought I was alone in these feelings. Then

300

I discovered several online forums where other female long-term cruising expressed their difficulties adjusting to their new lives on board. Can you imagine my relief? I was happy to discover that there were other women who were struggling. I was also happy to discover a variety of suggestions for how to manage these feelings. While some were useful and others slightly bizarre, the most important thing was that I had found a community.

As we have said several times in the book already, it takes time to transition to moving on to a boat and acknowledge the feelings associated with such change. I kept a journal of my feelings and I talked extensively with Leonard, and this enabled me to manage the change. In truth, I still struggle sometimes, with being a former teacher or a former counsellor and a current nothing except a vagabond, but I am getting there, slowly.

Pirate Queen or Home Bird?

To help you with your own transition to living on board, I have designed the following quiz. It's mainly a bit of fun, but it may also give you some insight into certain aspects of the cruising lifestyle and which of these aspects may need your attention before you depart.

1. **When you consider living on a boat do you...**
   a. Jump up and down with delight?
   b. Consider expanding your summer wardrobe, since you will never again need winter clothes?

---

c. Think 'Who in their right mind would live on a boat'?

d. Heave at the thought of it/get seasick in the bath?

2. **You've just seen your ideal boat on eBay but it needs some work. Do you...**

   a. Go directly online to check boat jumble – you love sorting through old stuff?

   b. Work out the cheapest way to renovate so you can flip it and buy a new boat?

   c. Erase the link in case your partner sees it?

   d. Start a conversation about extending your house?

3. **You have worked with your current company for 15 years and when you told them you were leaving they offered you a promotion and a raise. Do you...**

   a. Ring your partner and ask to defer your departure date for a year, so you can take the job?

   b. Daydream about your new office and decorating it?

   c. Tell the company 'Thanks but no thanks' and flounce off?

   d. Consider a way to start a similar internet-based business?

4. **You have been in your local musical society for 20 years and at the thought of leaving it behind, do you...**

   a. Do a little happy dance – you've wanted to leave for ages but never had the courage to do so?

   b. Feel a little sad but promise to post regularly on their Facebook page from whatever exotic location you happen to be visiting?

   c. Weep and mourn and wrap yourself around everyone in a great big hug before you leave?

   d. Get carried away at the going-away party and kiss everyone, wake up wondering what you've done, and try to bring forward your departure date for fear of meeting anyone at the supermarket?

5. **The local football club runs a fundraiser draw and you win the monthly first prize. You have a choice of...**

   a. A two-week self-catering holiday in a mobile home in France, including flights and car hire and £2,000 spending money.

   b. Two weeks in a villa in Turkey with a cook and maid, all expenses paid.

   c. A week in Disneyland, Florida, for the family, half board, and £1,000 spending money.

   d. £5,000 in cash.

6. **You're selling your house to move on to your boat full time when the deal falls through at the last minute. What is your reaction?**

   a. Relief – now you can ask for a little more, as next door has sold theirs for ten grand more than yours!

   b. Change estate agents and put it up for sale again.

   c. Just rent it out and get sailing already!

   d. Anxiety – you need the money to leave and now you will have to wait a little longer.

7. Your children are all grown up and leading their own lives. As you are about to leave your eldest daughter announces she is expecting a baby. Do you...

    a. Congratulate her and wish her well, offering any support you can give over email and social media apps?

    b. Call her as soon as possible and have some flowers delivered to her home at the earliest possible opportunity?

    c. Breathe a sigh of relief – you are useless at pregnancy and you and she rub each other up the wrong way anyway?

    d. Get involved in the passage planning so you can work out where you'll be around the time of the birth so you can book a flight home to see her and the new baby?

8. You have just had a pretty scary sail and you've been sick the whole time. Do you...

    a. Sit out in the cockpit where the sea air helps and you feel less sick?

    b. Sit in the cockpit and feel ill and moan to anyone who'll listen?

    c. Go below and take some medication for seasickness, have a little weep and pull yourself together?

    d. Go below and take some medication, and make some tea and bacon sandwiches for the crew, even though you still feel a little queasy?

9. **You and your partner have a huge fight and you're really cross. Do you...**
   a. Walk out of the boat and head to the ladies to sit and ring your friend and give out like hell about him?
   b. Book a flight home without telling him and head back for a few days?
   c. Buy a coffee, head to the laundrette for an hour, cool down, then go and find him and straighten it out?
   d. Go for a run and a swim and wait for him to apologise?

10. **You're in a remote anchorage when you get word that your elderly father has had a fall and has been admitted to hospital. Do you...**
   a. Ring your brother – he is the calmest sibling you have – and ask him how serious it is?
   b. Ring your daughter and ask her to go and see him in the hospital and to call you on video chat while she's there so you can see for yourself how he is doing?
   c. Do nothing, you haven't got a great relationship with him and he would much rather your sister and brother looked after him?
   d. Book a flight and go and see for yourself how he is doing?

To score the quiz, apply the number of points as shown below:

Q1 (a)4, (b)3, (c)2, (d)1. **Q2** (a)4, (b)3, (c)2, (d)1. **Q3** (a)2, (b)3, (c)4, (d)1. **Q4** (a)4, (b)3, (c)2, (d)1. **Q5** (a)1, (b)3, (c)2, (d)4. **Q6** (a)3, (b)2, (c)4, (d)1. **Q7** (a)2, (b)3, (c)1, (d)4. **Q8** (a)3, (b)1, (c)2, (d)4. **Q9** (a)2, (b)1, (c)4, (d)3. **Q10** (a)2, (b)4, (c)1, (d)3.

Results

30–40

You may well be on the way to becoming a Pirate Queen. You're ready to give up your job and role in the community. You have found a way to manage your family obligations and are well on the way to realising that life at sea is not all plain sailing, but you can manage it. You are enthusiastic about long-term cruising and can see your way to solving difficulties as they arise.

20–30

OK, you are enthusiastic and your heart may be in the right place. You're struggling in some areas – is it letting go of your home? Perhaps you could consider renting. Are you finding it hard to see yourself without a career? Have you considered retraining for something you can do from home or while you sail? Is it family or your local support network that is pulling at your heart strings? It is difficult to separate from people, but give yourself a chance and plan return visits if that's what you need. Long-term cruising is all about flexibility, so be flexible!

10–20

Oh gosh. You may be enthusiastic about the idea of living on a boat long term but you may have a bit more to do in letting go of your old life. But cheer up – everybody has to start somewhere!

Less than 10

You are most definitely a Home Bird. You are happy to be part of the great support networks for long-term cruisers and you're equally happy to see your friends follow their dreams, but you're not prepared to take the step of living on a boat full time. That's fair enough; you're very clear about who you are and what you want, and it is definitely not long-term cruising.

Fear

As I sit here in front of the computer, I know that I have a genuine struggle about the whole concept of fear and sailing. What is that struggle? I want to honour my experience of sailing with my family and the experience of lots of other women in a similar position, many of whom I have met personally or had contact with through social media. I also want to acknowledge two other realities: first, there may also be men out there who are terrified when they sail, but they are unable or unwilling to acknowledge that fear; and second, there are probably many women who are not fearful at all when they sail. Furthermore, in my experience it is a particular cohort of people I am describing, and that is cruisers who engage in offshore sailing with or without children on board.

Owning or chartering a boat with a group of mates and sailing in the Mediterranean or the Caribbean for your summer holidays with four or five other men or women is not quite the same thing as sailing with your family in your home, even if you're covering the same sailing ground. For one thing, you have four or five other adults on board and even if it's an inexperienced crew, you have access to adult minds with adult experience and critical thinking skills and competencies in a number of areas. If one or two, or even three, of the crew come down with seasickness, another 50 per cent are still capable. In a cruising family with two adults and two children you are already in a uniquely different situation.

On *Faoin Spéir*, Leonard is the skipper and the competent sailor. I am not a sailor, but I can sail the boat under direction. Luke and Ella are both capable of helming and doing a watch, which to date they have only done in the daytime. I am afflicted with night blindness, which I only discovered while night sailing. This reduces my ability to take a watch at night, which is a decided disadvantage in a two-adult crew. It certainly contributes to my being in a state of fear while I am sailing, but I think it is only one part of that and I want to explore the other elements of the fear and fear itself. I'm not sure that exploring the fear will actually remove it but I do think it will help me to manage it in some way.

When we became full-time liveaboards, we had very little experience of sailing in salt water. In fact, our first two sails in salt water were on *Faoin Spéir*. We set her in the water in Fenit Harbour in County Kerry and we sailed her to Bere Island along the Irish Atlantic Coast. We did the sail in two 45-mile hops with Ella on board. It was coastal sailing – we never left sight of land and we sailed out of Fenit on a beautiful summer morning in August doing approximately 1 knot in near windless conditions. Still, I was terrified; you can see it in my face in some of the old video footage.

The fear came from being in this tiny boat (relatively speaking), in a vast ocean, powerless, insignificant and at the mercy of the sea and the elements. I was not used to the boat, its motions or the impact of the sea and tidal flow on our vessel. It felt alien to me. I thought at any moment we were going to be tossed overboard and end up in the water, plunging to our deaths less than a mile offshore. Nobody would ever find us and we'd all be eaten by sharks and dolphins and fish and never again be seen! And worse still, Luke, who was not on board with us but playing football with his club, would be orphaned!

Do you see what happens? Fear leads to wild and out-of-control rantings of the imagination. This is the supreme art of turning a reasonable fear into a major drama with a view to soothing yourself so that you are justified in feeling what you feel. In reality, we were moving on an almost mirror-like sea on a boat that had crossed the North Atlantic Ocean in 30–40 knots of wind.

I'm not saying that all the fear and anxiety we feel when we sail is unfounded, as it most certainly is not. The sea is a powerful force and it behoves us to treat it with respect, to prepare our passages with regard for the weather, the tides and the capacity of the crew. However, I am saying that a little fear is a good thing; it makes us cautious and prevents us from being blasé. I also believe that fear in its own way is useful for keeping the mind focused.

Over the years we've had some hairy experiences sailing where I personally have been terrified, but I have had to suck it up and carry on because sailing is one of the few arenas remaining in modern life where there is not always an immediate solution. Sometimes you need to feel fear and carry on feeling it for several hours while you get the boat and crew safely to their destination or out of that particular tidal flow or squall. A good example was when we lost our helm on our first attempt at sailing the Scilly Isles. We were in no imminent danger and so had no need to contact the coastguard, and we returned to shore using the emergency tiller. Was it uncomfortable? Yes! Were we tossed about like a cork in a bath? Yes! Did we encounter other vessels and feel nervous about our interaction with them? Yes, yes and yes! I felt terror, genuinely, but I had to deal with it for seven hours and get on with it because expressing my fear was not helpful to the skipper and his assistant in getting back to shore, and it most certainly would not have helped my children to stay calm and manage the passage. Fear is present, it has a right to exist and is sometimes the correct response, but the luxury of expressing it or acting out of it can interfere with the focus of keeping everyone safe. Therefore, fear may be felt but not always heard.

Hair

I know hair colour may seem like a frivolous issue and I do beg the pardon of all those very serious and industrious sailors who have sailed their entire lives without the issue of hair colour ever raising its head. But the differences between weekend sailors and liveaboard cruisers are many and varied, and hair colour is one of those differences. Women who colour their hair and become liveaboard cruisers find themselves in something of a situation with regard to hair maintenance. I do not wish to take a sexist approach; it is possible that there are men out there who face the same issue and I wish to be an equal opportunities addresser on this matter. In truth, I raise it because it comes up as a regular subject on the long-term cruising online forums.

I myself was faced with a bit of a dilemma when I moved on board *Faoin Spéir* full time. I had thick, luxurious hair, dark in colour. The dark colour owed some of its lustre to hair dye.

But as I began to spend so much time in the outdoors on or close to the sea, my hair colour soon began to fade and look jaded. That was the first issue.

The second issue was in leaving Ireland, I also left behind my hairdresser who cut, styled and coloured my hair. Many women would agree that their hairdresser is akin to their doctor and finding a new one is difficult. You build up a relationship of trust with them; going to somebody else feels 'wrong' and it's never the same, no matter how good the new hairdresser is at their craft.

The third issue, of course, is water for washing. I have very thick hair and it needs quite an amount of water to wash and rinse it fully. There is never enough water on board *Faoin Spéir* for that, and most of the timed showers in marinas require the use of a second token at least to get a proper rinse.

Finally, there's the 'M' word: menopause. I was just starting the menopause as we began full-time cruising, and the quality and texture of my hair began to change. So what to do about all these issues concerning the hair and colouring it? I decided to go au naturel – to let the colour grow out and return to my own, natural colour.

Being perfectly honest, this was a tough decision and I almost lost courage several times. Whenever I would look in the mirror and see my grey roots I would get in a tizzy and think that I was too young for this, that I was letting myself go. As well as the pressure I put on myself, it came from family and friends, too. Although they're very supportive and caring people who I love very much and who I know love me, they told me straight that it didn't suit me to go grey and I should have a serious chat with myself and then book myself in for a colour. I ignored the comments, requests and advice, and instead I grew the colour out and went grey. The end result is that I am very happy with my decision and I feel my hair is healthy and in good condition as a result. Furthermore, it is more manageable as I cruise and does not cause me any problems whatsoever.

I am particularly curious about the struggle for me during this entire process. I consider myself a strong woman and pretty grounded in reality and immune to the pressures placed on us women by the beauty industry. I am comfortable with who I am and how I present – in fact, I have always been comfortable with myself. Whatever struggles I have had about myself and my image have been developmental and philosophical; for the most part, I am confident in my choices and decisions. But I really struggled with going grey. It challenged how I perceived myself and I began to see myself differently. People definitely have a strong reaction to it, but I guess I do too. This is very much who I am and I feel powerful saying that I am 52 years old and I have considerable life experience. I am not flaunting that or hiding it, I am simply acknowledging that I have the right to colour and style my hair the way I want it.

I know there are many more solutions to the hair-colour dilemma and you must seek out your own solution. Do what works for you and be confident in your decision, but never underestimate the power of grey!

Changing pace

I have succeeded in slowing down and in truth I must confess that boat life suits me. I consider *Faoin Spéir* to be home. It is the first real home Leonard and I have owned as a couple. We bought it together and it is renovated according to our taste. But our life as we travel the world on *Faoin Spéir* is truly remarkable. Slowing down means we have time for each other, we get to chat and hang out, talk and listen, argue, convince and defend, laugh, joke and share intimacy.

We developed a routine where we rise in the morning before the kids and we sit down and drink a pot of coffee, which Leonard usually makes. It is our preference to sit in the cockpit to drink our coffee and chat, although sometimes we adjourn to the dining area inside the boat because of the weather. It is indescribable to have this morning luxury. Sometimes I wonder if we'll run out of things to say to each other, and occasionally we do sit in silence and sip, because that is what suits us. On other occasions this silence is chosen because we're not in the mood for a chat, or possibly I am feeling a little grumpy and I don't want to talk. Whatever the soundtrack, this coffee-time ritual has become the civilising force of our day.

It is interesting that boat life takes on its own routine, and that this routine tends to be seasonal and dependent on where the focus of the day lies. The rest of our day is divided between education, chores, buying food and preparing meals, exercising and finding time to socialise and relax together. This is our routine if we are at anchor, moored or berthed. If we are setting sail, we prepare the boat and complete passage planning the night before and we try to have our coffee together in the morning before hauling anchor. The main thing is to stay calm, collected and connected to each other.

Our routine when we are staying put may seem very full, but in reality it takes place at a much slower pace than on land. However, because we don't have any modern conveniences on the boat, our lives are a little more labour-intensive than they would be back in Ireland. When available, we use marina or port bathroom facilities for showering, so this usually means a little trek to and fro, which adds more time to the morning ablutions. However, on the trek to the bathroom you're more likely to meet neighbours and friends. After coffee, when the kids get up we all have breakfast together (actually, we have all our meals together) and there is more chat. Mealtimes are a great chance for teaching and learning through sharing experience, considering the news headlines and discussing current affairs or issues.

Chores and tidying are next on the agenda and then we spend two hours in the process of formal education (see Chapter 11). Whichever of us is not teaching is usually writing and attending to business emails, Facebook or Twitter. After school, we eat lunch together and have room for more chat. The kids usually do the clean-up.

We don't have a fridge or car, so we usually do the shopping for dinner in the afternoon. This means a chance to combine exercise and the need to buy food with a little walk to the shop. I'm not a great fan of walking aimlessly, so walking to the shop suits me. The health benefits of exercise are obvious, but a less obvious benefit when you live on a boat is that it can become a little claustrophobic, so having the chance to get out and clear your head is extremely therapeutic.

In the afternoons, the kids take the opportunity to meet friends and either swim, kayak or sail – anything as long as it is outdoors and off the boat. If the weather is bad, we each find our own space on the boat and read or browse online. After dinner we usually have family time, either a film or a board game.

I think our life is very simple and straightforward. There are things that make it acceptable and things that make it unbearable. Access to Wi-Fi makes life comfortable for my children, and when we are without it, we find ourselves with a seething mass of teenagers! But lack of Wi-Fi also allows us to become creative and hang out together. It gives us more time to spend with each other and our friends.

Perhaps time is the greatest gift of our life on board. Obviously we have not created it, but by slowing everything down, we seem to have more time than others and have made choices about how best to use it.

Slowing down almost happens in spite of you. Moving the boat safely from A to B, you have to create the time to focus on the here and now. This has allowed us to leave our old life behind and it will allow you to do the same thing. While I still have occasional bouts of loneliness and miss my friends, my sisters and other family members, I recognise that the boat is now home. Productivity is still important to me and it takes time to make the adjustment, for you are leaving behind a lifetime of learning and internalising the messages from society. But it is a process of unlearning and accepting that it is OK to 'waste time' (because that is what it feels like in the beginning). Therefore, being patient and kind with yourself and those around you is the best way forwards. As a long-term cruiser, the likelihood is that you are very rich in time, the most valuable commodity in the world today. Take all the time you need and enjoy every single second.

18

Home comforts

(M) 'Home comforts' is such an interesting turn of phrase, I think. What does it conjure up for you? For me a home comfort is something, anything, that makes my life easier or more comfortable. Whatever that is for you, there is a strong likelihood that it does not exist on a sailboat. A sailboat is usually a compact vehicle that moves under sail. It is light and compact and the particular design of the hull and keel is what allows it to move with speed through the water. The shape of the hull and keel is also what makes the space inside the boat compact.

Physical space

The compact nature of a boat means that space is the first home comfort you'll likely miss when at sea. Lack of space affects your life on so many levels, which is hard to imagine before you become a cruiser. First, actual physical space. By this I mean the space to move around the boat. On *Faoin Spéir,* the kids have a cabin each and Leonard and I share a cabin, while the centre of the boat is the common space, galley, living room and bathroom. It is tight but really it only becomes an issue when we cannot get out due to bad weather. In good weather we also have the deck, which is quite large, and the cockpit, which is like an outdoor living room.

One of the ways we manage to create additional space is to find public places and other spaces *outside* of the boat. For example, if Leonard and I have a disagreement, we have to walk and talk outside of the boat so the kids cannot hear. Alternatively, we have to find an alternative space to sit and chat – that has varied from a hot tub in a gym to a coffee shop, laundrettes and a picnic table in a park. Our space becomes wherever we are at that moment in time.

Private space

Private space is a home comfort we are especially short on while living on the boat. Therefore, we have to create it when it is needed. In a house you take privacy for granted – you can go into a room and close the door and there it is. This does not happen on a boat; closing the door does not create silence or privacy. Privacy to sit and think has to be created and each individual has to create it for him or herself. I like to go and sit on the coach roof of the rear starboard quarter. It is possibly my favourite spot on the boat, but if we are tied alongside a quay or in a marina it is useless because of the passing traffic.

In addition to lacking space to think or argue in private there is also a lack of privacy for intimacy when you travel with two teenagers. This is not hugely problematic for us because, as a couple, Leonard and I are fine with being open and honest with each other. However, I can imagine that it could become an issue for couples who struggle to communicate. There are always solutions; the key is to seek them out.

In addition to all of the above the shared space in the boat is tiny and so it has to be used with consideration for the other people in the family. Everyone needs to keep their stuff tidy by putting it away after they have used it. I know this might seem mundane but in a boat tempers fray over those things that are easily dealt with on land in a larger house. In a tight space emotions can become overwhelming. It therefore requires awareness, effort and consideration to create space for yourself and your family at sea.

Storage space

Another way that space is affected on a boat is in limited storage space. It means there is only so much you can carry on board, therefore you will need to prioritise. Now I would like to say we can all survive with very little, and in truth we can. However, there is a big difference between weekend sailing and cruising long term as a life commitment. The former requires your holiday stuff to be used for a day or two until you get back to your real life, the latter *is* your life. Look around you right now and think about all the stuff you own and all of the things you use for everyday comfort and convenience. Imagine now you were asked to dispose of nine-tenths of it: what would you dispose of and what would you prioritise? Do not think of this as a 'desert island choice'. This is not what you would grab for survival; this is about living your life to the full with only a tenth of what you currently own.

Books, music, games and films can all be transported electronically, and electronics take up very little space on the boat; their only disadvantage is the power it takes to run them. But consider everything else: clothes, footwear, sports gear, bed linen, towels, cushions, glassware, crockery, cutlery, kitchen utensils, saucepans, medicine, toiletries, make-up ... the list goes on and on. All of this is before you even begin to consider safety equipment and sailing gear for the crew and boat. In our case it's all of that stuff for a family of four. What do you bring and what do you leave behind? Who decides and what process is used to make the decision? You must start by making decisions based on the space available, the boat's capacity and the crew's priorities.

Some inconvenient truths

Living the dream as a cruiser does mean that you must be willing to forgo many of the conveniences of land life. I suspect for each person who embraces the cruising life there are a specific set of conveniences, but what follows are the ones that crop up most often when I speak to cruisers and those of which I have personal experience.

Hot water on tap

For us, hot running water is a luxury, and one that I miss a great deal. I recognise that other boats have hot running water, so I do not wish to make a global point here. I just miss the simple pleasure of being able to turn on the tap and have hot water flow out. Now I know that this is a first-world problem, but there we go. We do of course have access to hot water in the bathrooms or the laundries of marinas, or we heat water on the boat in a kettle, but it takes work and is slightly inconvenient.

A washing machine

I miss having a washing machine of my own. Washing clothes is not a problem – we can all soak and hand wash – but washing bed linen, towels and tea towels is a bit more complex. In the winter we use laundrettes and laundry facilities in the marina for washing and drying clothes, but in the summer we hand wash and we dry on the lifelines.

I miss the convenience of having a washing machine, the ease of being able to gather laundry and use laundry detergent and load the washing machine and not have to think about it again until it's done. Pure bliss! Now, I admit to having a bit of a thing for laundry – it soothes me. I know it's a bit weird but before you get all judgemental, it is less destructive than alcohol or tobacco – less fun, too, I know, but that's the way it is. I like the smell of newly laundered clothes. I like sorting them, folding them and returning them in neat piles to the owners. It gives me a deep sense of accomplishment and satisfaction. It is not quite as satisfying without the washing machine, actually it is more work! Carrying the dirty laundry to the laundrette and dragging it all back again is just a chore sometimes. I can only imagine how much more difficult it might be with a small baby or children on board.

Heat on demand

Is there anything more luxurious than sitting in a soft chair in front of a coal fire on a cold, wet and miserable winter's evening? It is the essence of home comfort as far as I am concerned. Perhaps it's because we've done most of our cruising so far in the northern hemisphere and in the winter it has been cold, with temperatures as low as -6°C, but I seriously miss it.

We have soft chairs on the boat, but you could not call them sofas. We don't have a heating system on the boat, so it can get cool or even cold in the winter. Instead we use bioethanol, which we burn in a metal container. It is definitely not a coal fire but it is a flame that heats without a smell, so it's cosy and it does not contribute to condensation, which is a very significant factor when you live on a plastic boat. In extreme circumstances and when we have access to shore electricity we also use a 2kw fan heater. It works quite well, as it heats the space in the boat quickly. So we have heat, but it is the comfort of the fire that is missing.

The bath

I love a long soak in a bath; it's good for the body, the mind and the soul. It allows for relaxation and soothing away the aches and pains of daily living. I know it is a bit old-fashioned nowadays, as many people embrace the pleasure and rapidity of the power shower, but a bath is restorative and practical, in my opinion. It is probably one of the home comforts I miss the most. We do have a bath on board but without the water capacity to soak, it is less effective.

In the first year that we were cruising we spent the winter in Gillingham, just outside London. As berth holders in the marina, we had access to the leisure centre there and it had a hot tub. It was a little piece of heaven. I loved it. It had all the healing power of a bath and in addition it was a great place in which to chat to people and get to know the locals. I think the experience I had there would lead me to consider forking out for a session at a leisure centre just for the soothing experience of a hot tub.

The car

I am going to include the car as a home comfort. As somebody who has driven and had access to a car all of my adult life, I miss this too. It's not that I miss the particular car I was driving before we left, or any particular car for that matter, but it is the convenience and the ease with which it allows one to move about and plan. I miss using the car for shopping; without one, we only buy what we can carry and is necessary for that day. However, this does enable us to stick to our daily budget and to get exercise through walking. In addition, we lower our carbon footprint and we have no car expenses. But nonetheless I miss the car, because when I have one or access to one it makes my life easier and more comfortable.

19

Staying in touch

M When we decided to cruise we spent quite a bit of time researching how to stay in touch with family and friends. Staying connected is vitally important. Some people may look at this as an unwillingness to commit to cruising and make the leap into the unknown. I disagree; there are times when we are off grid and unavailable, but when and where we can, we stay in touch. As adults we have enough life experience to realise that friendships and family connections are capable of surviving separation, but staying in touch is very important, especially for the kids.

When we spoke to cruisers like Bill and Laurel Cooper or the couple who owned the boat before us they all mentioned how letter writing and long-distance phone calls had allowed them to maintain regular contact with their loved ones at home. That was indeed their reality.

Our reality is very different. Modern communications have greatly enhanced the ease with which we can stay in touch. While still 'long distance', we make calls via mobile phones several miles offshore. No longer is there a need to fill a pay phone with coins by the kilo to make an international call. Email is, of course, free and instant, with an always open inbox that acts as a virtual postal address.

Luke and Ella are digital natives, meaning they have grown up with technology and computers as a first language. They have never known a world without the internet. When we first talked about cruising they were initially incredulous and later resistant. Their resistance was due in large measure to the unavoidable separation from friends and family. At the time they did not own a personal mobile phone, as I was reluctant to provide one for them, fearing the disadvantages more than the advantage of owning such a device at a young age. It was my belief that they were unnecessary, as my children were either with me or with other adults entrusted with their care who were capable of contacting me in the event of an emergency. I also held, and continue to hold, the belief that parents need to protect their children from some of the negative aspects of the internet until they have acquired the skills and knowledge to negotiate it and the vast array of people who use it, good and bad. These reasons resulted in my decision to leave Luke and Ella without personal mobiles until their 12th birthday (a year before we set off).

Mobile phones

Today, each of us has a mobile phone on board *Faoin Spéir* and this is primarily how we keep in touch with friends and family. The particular phones we have are unlocked dual SIM mobiles. They can hold two SIM cards concurrently and usually we have our home SIM cards and a SIM from the country in which we're living at the time. The advantage of this is we can receive calls and texts from home for very little cost (typically less than 1p per minute) or on data roaming, while the domestic SIM card allows us to access data in the country in which we're residing.

Email and letters

Email has completely transformed the way cruisers send and receive letters. Without the need for a physical address, we are able to send email from any place with an internet connection, and with satellite telephony, this means *anywhere.*

It even helps with receiving traditional post on the move, too. It is a rare occurrence, but if a piece of mail arrives for us in Ireland (usually something official), we have someone open it, scan it and email it to us. Within minutes we can have a printout in our hands. If it's a form of some sort, we can print it, fill it out, rescan the completed form and email it back to the sender. Fortunately, the need for this process is very rare, as most officialdom has moved into the virtual realm.

I quite enjoy letter writing. I believe it to be a lost art and I love nothing more than the pleasure of receiving a personal letter in the post. For this, we use marina addresses when we can. We have never encountered a marina or yacht club that would not oblige in receiving and holding post for us. When my mother was alive I wrote to her regularly from the boat. I like letters because they are personal and intimate, and there is no possibility of them ending up in the public arena unless the recipient shares them. Sending a letter while cruising is as easy as sending a postcard while on holiday.

Social media

We use a variety of data-based social media and messaging apps to keep in touch with family and friends. Messaging apps in particular have been used to great effect by all on board. In an instant, you can send a short text message, a photograph, video or document to another user of the same service, and there is no additional charge beyond your data connection. If your connection is good enough you can even have face-to-face video conversations via these apps. I am slow to name any, as the app world seems to move so rapidly, but there are a few that have stood the test of time, including Skype, WhatsApp and Facebook Messenger.

AIS

We have already mentioned just how useful an AIS transponder is on the boat when sailing. The signal we put out, with our position, speed and bearing, is not only picked up by other boats but also by land-based receiving stations. Some of these then relay the received information via the internet to services like MarineTraffic and VesselFinder. These services then plot your information, and that of all other shipping around the world, on to an interactive online map. Anyone can type our boat name into one of these sites and it will show them exactly where we are. Occasionally, if we are too far offshore, then we disappear, but the technology will give our last-received transmission.

Staying in touch in the 'analogue world'

The cruising life can be a struggle sometimes because, as a parent, it is my job to help my children develop the life skills that will allow them to live a healthy and wholesome life, and I do believe that developing the ability to manage loneliness is essential to a balanced life. When loneliness pops up its head I encourage my children to acknowledge it and feel it and cry a little if that helps, and certainly to chat about how they feel. I definitely do not want them

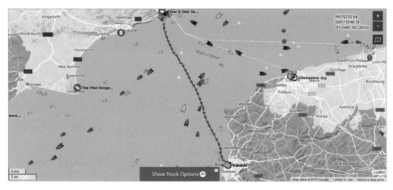

A screengrab from www.marinetraffic.com of our friends on *S/V Duma* at the time of writing. Reproduced with the kind permission of MarineTraffic.

to pretend it is not there or, worse, still be fearful of it and become engaged in the process of trying anything and everything to avoid the feeling. To behave in such a way gives the feeling of loneliness a power it ought never possess.

Staying in touch via digital means is all well and good, but sometimes what is really needed is a visit home, or a visit from the people at home. It is important to us but we have found it to be essential for the kids. It allows them peace of mind and to be able to let go and live the cruising lifestyle to the full, in the knowledge that if they miss home too much, we'll do our best to facilitate a visit.

Low-cost airlines

We often take advantage of the low-cost air carriers to return to Ireland for a proper catch-up with family and friends. Timed right, you can fly almost anywhere in Europe for about £20.

Family visits

Further to our popping home regularly courtesy of budget airlines, we are fortunate enough to have regular visits from friends and family. These visits bestow great joy but they come with several other advantages, too. First, they allow our friends to see that the cruising lifestyle brings with it many benefits; primarily, it is adaptable and so allows for time to be spent enjoying the company of others.

Second, and one of the benefits I quite enjoy, is they allow the people we love to see that we do in fact have a fairly regular life, with routine and discipline, and that we take the home education aspect of cruising very seriously.

The cruising life affords many advantages in all aspects of life, but primarily it gives us the opportunity to be creators of the life we desire. Staying in touch and fostering the bonds of friendship and family in person and through electronic communication has proven to be far less difficult in the modern world.

20

In the end

L The question of duration came up many times before we set off. How long would we be gone? When would we next return? Each time I said that I was going 'for good'. I really did see myself sailing all the way to the grave, which I hope is very far away.

Having got to the place where we are living and sailing on *Faoin Spéir*, I feel like that question is now much more open-ended. Achieving what seemed impossible has opened my eyes to all the other 'impossibilities' and left me wondering what's next. For now, all I can say for certain is that I'm not done sailing about the world, and I may never be, but every day I remain open to the idea that my tomorrow may be completely different to anything I dreamed today, and I'm sure that it will suit me very well.

At the time of writing, we are in France and mid-preparation for another season. I'm watching the other sailboats out for a Sunday sail and wishing that we were already underway. We are readying ourselves and the boat to head ever further from our home shores – I've always fancied a winter in Cape Verde. Although I look forward to the voyage, the beauty of being a liveaboard cruiser is that I cannot say for certain we will get there, or if we do, that we will winter there. We may just find a little piece of paradise in some Moroccan riad and decide to live out the rest of our lives there. I doubt it, but if I've learned anything from a life afloat, it's that you cannot depend on a cruising sailor to be where they say they will be, when they say they will be there.

On our journey thus far we have had the good fortune to meet many couples and families who have gone before us, each more generous with their time, advice and even spares than the last. When asked about how they felt about the liveaboard cruising lifestyle, not a single one ever mentioned regret. They often spoke of difficult periods, of times they would have liked to have reached port sooner or simply to have devoured a slice of fresh cream sponge. But never regret.

Now that we are out 'doing it', I have to say that there is not a part of me that regrets setting out on a sailboat. It is every bit as amazing as I had imagined, although many things are different from our expectations when we first sat around the kitchen table making our plan. We have not yet made it to sunny climes, yet the adventure and excitement was as great reaching each new port as it might be arriving halfway around the world. It has not always been easy. There have been times where it looked like we had reached a brick wall and would have to postpone, if not abandon, the project. But each day, we did a little bit more and each day it became more real.

Of course there are many little things that I would do differently if I were to start again and almost all of these are related to practicalities, things like ensuring that I had run *all* of the necessary in-mast cables before stepping the mast. Many of these small things are not worth stressing about and are lessons learned along the way. If I could only pick one thing that I would have done differently, then it is simply that I would have done it sooner.

When I meet others tempted by the lure of escaping under sail, I always think of Éamonn and Rebecca of *Wayward* and when we first met. Their advice was: 'Just go; you'll never regret it.'

Useful resources

Books

Faoin Spéir's favourites

A World of My Own, Robin Knox-Johnston (Adlard Coles, 2013)

Reeds Weather Handbook for Sail and Power, Frank Singleton (Thomas Reed, 2014)

Replacing Your Boat's Electrical System, Mike Westin (Adlard Coles, 2013)

Sailing Alone Around the World, Joshua Slocum (Adlard Coles, 2006)

Sell Up and Sail, 5th ed., Bill and Laurel Cooper (Adlard Coles, 2005)

The Adlard Coles Book of Diesel Engines, 4th ed., Tim Bartlett (Adlard Coles, 2011)

The Adlard Coles Book of Knots, Peter Owen (Adlard Coles, 2006)

The Long Way, revised ed., Bernard Moitessier (Rowman & Littlefield, Sheridan House, 1995)

A Voyage for Madmen, Peter Nichols (Harper Collins, 2009)

Seamanship

Celestial Navigation for Yachtsmen, 13th ed., Mary Blewitt (Adlard Coles, 2017)

Hand, Reef and Steer, Tom Cunliffe, 2nd ed., (Adlard Coles, 2016)

Heavy Weather Sailing, 7th ed., Peter Bruce (Adlard Coles, 2016)

Metal Corrosion in Boats, Nigel Warren (Adlard Coles, 2006)

RYA VHF Handbook (G31), Tim Bartlett (RYA, 2006)

RYA Navigation Handbook, Tim Bartlett (RYA, 2014)

RYA Handy Guide to Marine Radio (inc. GDMSS) (E22), (RYA, 2018)

RYA VHF Radio SRC Syllabus and Sample Exam Questions (EG 26), (RYA, 2012)

Safe Skipper: A Practical Guide to Managing Risk at Sea, Simon Jollands & Rupert Holmes (Adlard Coles, 2015)

The Rigging Handbook, Brion Toss (Adlard Coles, 2004)

Sailing competency

Competent Crew, 5th ed., Pat Langley-Price & Philip Ouvry (Adlard Coles, 2007)

Pass Your Day Skipper, 6th ed., David Fairhall (Adlard Coles, 2017)

Reeds Crew Handbook, Bill Johnson (Adlard Coles, 2012)

Reeds Skipper Handbook, 6th ed., Malcolm Pearson (Adlard Coles, 2010)

The Adlard Coles Book of the International Certificate of Competence, Bill Anderson (Adlard Coles, 2010)

The Complete Day Skipper, 5th ed., Tom Cunliffe (Adlard Coles, 2016)

The Complete Yachtmaster, 6th ed., Tom Cunliffe (Adlard Coles, 2017)

Blue Water Cruising

Dream Cruising Destinations, Vanessa Bird (Adlard Coles, 2015)

Ocean Passages and Landfalls, Rob Heikell & Andy O'Grady (Imray, 2009)

The Voyager's Handbook, 2nd ed., Beth Ann Leonard (McGraw Companies Publishing, 2007)

World Cruising Routes, Jimmy Cornell (Adlard Coles, 2014)

World Voyage Planner, Jimmy Cornell (Adlard Coles, 2012)

Your First Atlantic Crossing, Les Weatheritt (Adlard Coles, 2014)

Health

Advanced First Aid Afloat, Peter F. Eastman (Cornell Maritime, 2009)

Doctor on Board, Dr Jürgen Hauert (Sheridan House, 2010)

First Aid Afloat: Instructional Guide for Handling Emergencies the Correct Way, Fabian Steffan (Cornell Maritime, 2014)

Where There Is No Doctor: A Village Health Care Handbook, revised ed., David Werner & Carol Thuman (Macmillan Education, 2004)

Where There Is No Dentist, Murray Dickson (The Hesperian Foundation, 1983)

Cookery

Field Guide to Seafood, Aliza Green (Quirk Publications, 2007)

Reeds Cooking at Sea Handbook, Sonja Brodie (Adlard Coles, 2017)

Dictionaries

The Illustrated Boat Dictionary in 9 Languages (Adlard Coles, 2014)

Yachtman's Ten Language Dictionary, Barbara Webb (Adlard Coles, 2008)

Education

A Charlotte Mason Education: A Homeschooling How-to Manual, Catherine Levinson (Champion Press Ltd, 2000)

Finding Your Element, Ken Robinson & Lou Aronica (Penguin Publishing, 2014)

How to Raise an Amazing Child The Montessori Way, 2nd ed., Tim Seldin (DK Publications, 2006)

Teach Your Own: *The John Holt Book of Homeschooling*, John Holt, Pat Farenga (De Capo Publishing, 2003)

The Unschooling Handbook, Mary Griffith (Prima Publishing, 1998)

Waldorf Education: An Introduction for Parents, Ed. David
 Mitchell (Waldorf Publications, 2016)
You, Your Child and School, Ken Robinson & Lou Aronica
 (Penguin Publishing, 2018)

Websites

Sailing websites

www.asa.com
www.collisionregs.com
www.imo.org
www.marine-education.eu
www.maritimeskillsacademy.com
www.sailing.ca
www.sailing.org.au
www.theca.org.uk
www.trinityhouse.co.uk

Sailing magazines

www.goodoldboat.com
www.sailbuyersguide.com
www.ybw.com

Weather websites

www.nhc.noaa.gov (National Hurricane Center, a division
 of the US National Weather Service)

www.passageweather.com

www.weather.gov (US government site for weather prediction)

www.windy.com

Navigation

www.bookharbour.com (Chart suppliers Internationally, Imray and Admiralty)

www.admiralty.co.uk/maritime-safety-information/ admiralty/notices-to-mariners (Notices to mariners for UK charts)

www.pcmaritime.com

www.rin.org.uk (Royal Institute of Navigation)

Health

www.crewmedic.com (Marine first aid kits)

www.dentanurse.com (Dental repair and first aid kits)

www.fitfortravel.nhs.uk/home

www.gov.uk/foreign-travel-advice

www.thehealthatoz.com

www.iamat.org (International Association for Medical Assistance to Travellers)

www.masta-travel-health.com (Travel advice for travellers)

Home education

www.aussieeducator.org.au (official Australian government site) www.gov.uk (UK guidelines)

www.homeschool.ie (Irish home schooling site)

www.homeschoolmedia.net (Home schooling in Canada)

www.hslda.org (US site with international information on home schooling)

www.state.gov (US government's official site for home schooling)

Examinations

www.examinations.ie (Irish State Examinations Commission)

www.ibo.org (International Baccalaureate, outlines the curriculum and all associated requirements to complete the examination)

www.nidirect.gov.uk/information-and-services/14-19-education-employment-and-training-options/coursework-and-exams (Information on A-levels, which are recognised internationally)

Resources for home schooling

www.bbc.co.uk/schools/parents/home_education (A wide variety of high-quality resources for home schooling)

www.bbc.com/education/subjects

www.bbc.co.uk/learning

www.thecanadianhomeschooler.com (Materials for home schooling in Canada)

www.homeschool.com/resources/americanschool (Resources suitable for home schooling the US curriculum) www.home-ed.vic.edu.au/resources (Home Education Network – an Australian website dedicated to helping parents navigate the issue of what to teach and ways to find material)

General education

www.open.edu/openlearn/free-courses (Open University free courses)

Yachting clubs and organisations

www.cruising.org.uk
www.oceancruisingclub.org
www.rya.org.uk
www.ssca.org

Cruise in company rallies

www.worldcruising.com (ARC, ARC Europe)
www.yachtrallies.co.uk (Blue Water Rally)

Book websites

www.adlardcoles.com
www.bookfinder.com
www.bookharbour.com
www.fishernauticalbooks.co.uk

Search and rescue

www.irishlifeboats.com
www.rnli.org (Royal National Lifeboat Institution, UK)
www.dco.uscg.mil (US Coast Guard)

Generally useful websites

www.force4.co.uk (UK online chandlery)
www.icc-ccs.org (Up-to-date statistics on maritime piracy)
www.thechandleryonline.com

Acknowledgements

Although the *Faoin Spéir* project has centred around her crew of four, Leonard, Mary, Luke and Ella, her tribe extends around the globe. To say that it wouldn't have been possible without the help and support of this tribe would be clichéd, and if you've read the book, you'll find that clichés are something that we try to avoid. So, let us simply say that without the Faoin Spéir tribe, it all may well have been too difficult.

To the family who are not aboard, but are with us every day of our journey – Richard Kelly and David Skinner – your faith, support and love are felt in every mile under the keel.

There are a handful of people who have made their time, expertise, resources and friendship available to us, as though it was they who were slipping the lines: Rachel and Patrick Harrington of Lawrence Cove Marina in Bere Island, Garrett 'Super Chandler' Kelly from Union Chandlery, John Skinner, John Sinnott, and Stephen and Jan Chambers.

For the long conversations late into the night, and the advice, ideas and camaraderie of fellow dreamers, much gratitude and love goes out to Jim Rueff & Linda Davis, Robin & Sam King, Ian Cunningham, Robert Crane,

Acknowledgements

Jodie Kettridge & Thomas Crane, Éamonn O'Carroll & Becky Santos, Thierry Henrotte-Bois and Eric Ciré.

There are many ways of contributing to a project like *Faoin Spéir* and our heartfelt thanks go out to Peter & John Lawless, Greg Harvey & Family, and Wietse Buwalda from Salve Marine for your warmth and kindness. To Vin & Amy Gallagher from Sailing Nervous, Aodhan O'Ferrell, Jeremiah & Brittany Gowl from Lazy Gecko Sailing, Emily McGann, Andrew Ryan, Daniel Culpepper, Jon Jeter, Kacey Cramer, Jack & Julie Andrys, and all of those who regularly follow, like, subscribe and send kind words in the virtual ocean. We thank you for making it all a little easier.

When it came to creating the book, Stephen King said it best when he wrote, 'to write is human, to edit is divine.' And so, to the saints at Bloomsbury; Jenny Clark, Eleanor Lee and Jonathan Eyers. Sincerely, this book owes a great deal to their efforts, patience and supreme professionalism.

Index

Index

Index

Index